ISO 9000
Worldwide Quality Standard

James G. Patterson

A FIFTY-MINUTE™ SERIES BOOK

CRISP PUBLICATIONS, INC.
Menlo Park, California

ISO 9000
Worldwide Quality Standard

James G. Patterson

CREDITS
Editor: **Janis Paris**
Typesetting: **ExecuStaff**
Cover Design: **Carol Harris**
Artwork: **Ralph Mapson**

Copyright © 1995 by Crisp Publications, Inc.
Printed in the United States of America by Bawden Printing Company.

http://www.crisp-pub.com

Distribution to the U.S. Trade:

National Book Network, Inc.
4720 Boston Way
Lanham, MD 20706
1-800-462-6420

99 00 01 02   10 9 8 7 6 5 4 3 2

Library of Congress Catalog Card Number 93-74236
Patterson, James G.
ISO 9000
ISBN 1-56052-291-7

This book is printed on recyclable paper with soy ink.

LEARNING OBJECTIVES FOR:

ISO 9000

The objectives for *ISO 9000* are listed below. They have been developed to guide you, the reader, to the core issues covered in this book.

Objectives

- ❏ 1) **To explain decision making about ISO 9000 certification**

- ❏ 2) **To discuss the process of ISO certification**

- ❏ 3) **To present certain ISO 9000 requirements and to comment on them**

Assessing Your Progress

In addition to the learning objectives, Crisp, Inc. has developed an **assessment** that covers the fundamental information presented in this book. A twenty-five item, multiple choice/true-false question-naire allows the reader to evaluate his or her comprehension of the subject matter. An answer sheet with a chart matching the questions to the listed objectives is also available. To learn how to obtain a copy of this assessment, please call **1-800-442-7477** and ask to speak with a Customer Service Representative.

Assessments should not be used in any selection process.

ABOUT THE AUTHOR

James Gordon Patterson, known as "The Cogent Communicator," is a trainer, speaker, and consultant on communication and management issues. In addition, he is a professor of communication, management, and computer information systems at the University of Phoenix and an education specialist with the United States Army.

Jim has written articles on communication and management issues for *Management World, The Toastmaster, Sound Management,* and *The Military Intelligence Magazine.* His American Society for Training and Development "Info-Line" book, *Fundamentals of Leadership,* was the Society's February 1994 selection.

Jim received his M.A. in organizational communication from Eastern Michigan University and his B.A. in journalism and international relations from the University of Arizona. He has done advanced graduate work in business, communication, and adult education at the University of Arizona and is currently working on a second Master's degree in organizational behavior from the University of London's Birkbeck College.

Jim is a member of the International Society for Performance Improvement (ISPI) and the United States Air Force Civil Air Patrol (CAP).

Contact Jim at:

James Gordon Patterson
9571 East Caldwell Drive
Tucson, Arizona 85747-9218
E-mail: *Cogent@flash.net*
Web Address: *http://teacher.uophx.edu/jgpatter*

ABOUT THIS BOOK

After reading this book, based on the most recent changes to ISO 9000 Series approved for 1994, you'll have a greater understanding of what it takes to get ISO 9000 certification. Learn why getting certified to an ISO 9000 quality standard will give your company an added marketing tool, making you competitive in the European Economic Community and the world. Discover how just going through the ISO 9000 process will revolutionize your company for the better. Find out how adopting ISO 9000 will give you the stucture to make total quality management more effective. Here are just a few of the benefits that come from ISO 9000 certification: you can save money and improve productivity through a drastic drop in reworking products, improve employees' morale and reduce stress through an emphasis on teamwork, and prove to your customers the processes you use are under control—saving them the expense of having to audit each of their suppliers independently. Finally, just going through the ISO 9000 process forces you to take a hard look at everything you do in your business.

ACKNOWLEDGMENTS

I'd like to thank the following people for their help on this book:

Professor Alex Dely, Tucson Transatlantic Trade and Chapman College, for his wealth of articles and sources.

W. Dean Hawley, president of Attexor, N.A., for his tremendous insight into the elements of ISO 9001.

The research staffs at both the American Society for Training and Development and the American Society for Quality Control for providing excellent bibliographies.

Dedication

This book is dedicated to my late father, James G. "Doc" Patterson, Jr., an old Army Air Corps mess sergeant, a proud graduate of Concord (MI) High School and two weeks of fire prevention school at Michigan State, and a man smarter than any Ph.D. I ever knew. He taught me if a job's worth doing, it's worth doing right (*and to keep my nose clean and keep regular*).

CONTENTS

ISO 9000

INTRODUCTION

What Is ISO 9000?

It has to do with that quality thing. We've had the Malcolm Baldrige National Quality Award, the Deming Award, Kaizen, TQM . . . now it's ISO 9000. Is it a passing fad or does it have some real value? ISO, from the International Standards Organization based in Geneva, Switzerland, is not an acronym, according to John Swaelens of the Geneva-based *ISO 9000 News*—the term actually means *equal.* The objective of ISO is to ease international trade through the development of world standards for systems, products, and services. If your company has achieved an ISO 9000 system registration, you can make the legitimate claim you have a documented *quality system* that you've effectively implemented and consistently followed. What certification does *not* mean is that your product or service has any quality.

What ISO 9000 Certification Is Not

ISO 9000 is a *quality* system standard, *not* a *technical product* standard. Certification to a particular ISO 9000 series does not put a registrar's stamp of approval on your product or service. All certification says is that your quality processes are in order, that you actually do what you say you do.

If you do get ISO 9000 certification, you can rightfully tell your customers you have a documented quality system you've implemented and consistently follow. Obviously, if you follow your quality processes, chances are high you will produce quality products and services.

But what you can't advertise is that your ISO 9000 certification means you have a quality product or service. If you do, your registrar is likely to take away your certification!

SECTION

I

The ISO 9000 Series

*"Quality does not happen by accident;
it has to be planned."*

—Joseph M. Juran

ISO . . . THE WAVE OF THE FUTURE

The International Standards Organization is a worldwide federation founded in 1946 to promote world standards for manufacturing, trade, and communication and is made up of member bodies of some 90 countries. The American National Standards Institute (ANSI) is the U.S. representative to ISO. ISO develops standards in all industries except electrical and electronic engineering. Standards in these areas are made by the Geneva-based International Electrotechnical Commission, which is made up of representatives from more than 40 countries, including the United States.

The United States has adopted the ISO 9000 series as the ANSI/ASQC (American Society for Quality Control) Q90 series (Q90, Q91, Q92, and Q93). In the United Kingdom, the ISO 9000 is called BS 5750. The European Community calls ISO 9000 European Norm (EN) 29000.

Sound confusing? It really isn't. To better understand what ISO 9000 quality is all about, let's look at a familiar process we all go through: getting our car oil changed:

Quality in Everyday Life: An ISO 9000 Parable

Your quality adventure starts when you drive in to an oil-change shop and the person at the front desk asks if you have any discount coupons. No coupon? Here you go! Then the guy says your car will be ready in 15 minutes.

While waiting for your car you wonder what else the repair people will find wrong with your car. How much more will it cost? How much longer will it take? This is what ISO 9000 is all about—your confidence that the job will be done right and on time as promised. This quality standard demands attention be paid at every step along the way to changing your oil, or whatever other problems the repair people will fix in your car.

You picked this place to bring your car because you've seen the shop on the corner for years and you've heard good things about it . . . people say it is a quality shop.

ISO . . . THE WAVE OF THE FUTURE (continued)

The way the clerk took your order made you feel confident the shop has procedures to handle this kind of thing. They don't appear to be making it up as they go along. You also hope the mechanic has gotten the training to know how to change the oil in your particular car with the right kind of filter and will follow some kind of procedure to check your windshield wipers, tires, spark plugs, and all the other widgets that make your car run safely. You also have confidence that if the mechanic picked up a part to put in your car to replace one that was defective, he'd separate that discarded bad part from the good ones so it wouldn't wind up in somebody else's car. You also expect the mechanics will do the job right without having to do it over again. In fact, after they finish the job, they hand you a checklist of all the things they did to your car.

Finally, although that oil change shop didn't have to do it, they offered you a free car wash.

This example* pretty much encompasses the 20 major quality elements covered in ISO 9001 that you'll find covered later in this book.

ISO 9000 is already popular in Europe, where more than 25,000 ISO 9000 certificates have been issued out of a total of more than 30,000 worldwide. In the United States, there were over 2,000 certifications by the end of 1993, and some estimate that over 5,000 certificates will be issued by the end of 1994.

Yet many North American business leaders still ask, "What the heck is an ISO?"

ISO 9000 is actually a series of five documents, ISO 9000 through ISO 9004, that describe the requirements for a quality management system. The standards, explained later in the book, are intentionally generic. They describe universal requirements and aren't product or industry specific. This is an important distinction: ISO 9000 series quality standards are flexible enough to adjust to your particular industry and management style. The standards also apply to all kinds of companies, large and small, in both the service and manufacturing sectors. If you are ISO 9000 series certified, the certification tells customers you do what you say you do and you can document it. Nothing more; nothing less.

---

*Rabbitt, John T. and Peter A. Bergh. *The ISO 9000 Book*, White Plains, NY: AMACOM Books, 1993. Adapted with permission.

ISO GIVES YOU A COMPETITIVE EDGE

If you're currently exporting or thinking about competing worldwide, conformance to ISO 9000 standards will put you on an even playing field with your competitors. Since the European Community with its 320 million-plus consumers has adopted ISO 9000, it may be required in the future for sales in Europe. In the United States, the U.S. Food and Drug Administration (FDA) intends to incorporate ISO 9000 standards in its Good Manufacturing Practices (GMP) regulations for medical devices. The Department of Energy (DOE) is also considering using the ISO 9000 series. If you do business with the U.S. Department of Defense, you'll soon see a switch from MIL-Q-9858a (Military Quality Standards) to ISO 9000. If you're a supplier with any of the Fortune 1000, chances are good you've heard noises they'll soon ask you to be ISO 9000 certified. Even now, it if comes down to two comparable vendors, you and the one who is ISO 9000 certified, the company with the ISO 9000 certificate will often get the business.

It isn't just government regulations that drive ISO 9000 certification; it's customers. ISO 9000 was originally developed for two-party contractual situations to satisfy the customer's quality assurance requirements and increase the customer's confidence in the quality systems of its suppliers. ISO 9000 series certification eliminates all the costly multiple on-site vendor quality audits of the past.

Many other companies are implementing ISO 9001, 9002, or 9003 because it is a legal requirement in certain industries to enter a particular marketplace or because it helps meet national regulations.

Some companies get ISO 9000 series certification in part for product liability defense. The existence of a documented quality system may minimize liability claims.

Even if you don't think you'll ever do business overseas, ISO 9000 is a great opportunity to establish a quality system. If you're practicing total quality management (TQM), already operating under MIL-Q standards, or have done work toward the Malcolm Baldrige Award in your business, you're halfway to ISO 9000 (in fact, you're better off preparing for ISO 9000 series certification first, then the Baldrige Award). If you want to institute TQM, ISO 9000 is a great place to start. Why? It forces you to take a good hard look at the processes you use to build a quality product or service. Preparing for ISO 9000 certification prods you to create more employee involvement and encourages understanding of quality systems at work in your company.

ISO GIVES YOU A COMPETITIVE EDGE (continued)

ISO 9000 certification is by facility, not by company. Your facility becomes certified when you show your quality system meets ISO 9000 standards in terms of documentation and performance. An accredited organization recognized by the country where you intend to do business does the certifying through reviewing your facility's quality manual to ensure it meets the particular ISO 9000 standard and by auditing your company's processes to ensure that the system documented in the quality manual is in place and effective. Certification normally lasts three years with the registrar conducting unannounced audits of your facility about every six months to make sure you continue to meet the standard.

According to Dan Dubbs of the *Facilities Design and Management* magazine, the person chosen to audit and register a company to an ISO 9000 series standard can be more important than the certificate itself. Anyone can say he or she is an ISO 9000 registrar. But not everybody is accredited to do so. In the United States, accreditation comes from a joint program of the Registrar Accreditation Board (RAB) and the American National Standards Institute (ANSI). Most other nations have similar accrediting bodies. The key here is to make sure the registrar you pick to audit and grant you certification is accredited by RAB/ANSI or some similar national body recognized by the country or countries targeted for your product or service. Also, the registrar you pick must have experience in your organization's primary business.

ISO 9000 is quality management oriented. It provides for quality and the improvement of quality. It may not be mandated by law yet, but it is one way to meet regulatory requirements and is an accepted practice of how to maintain quality.

ISO 9000 CERTIFICATION . . . DO YOU HAVE WHAT IT TAKES?

WHAT DOES IT TAKE?

To make ISO 9000 happen in your organization, it takes total commitment of top-level leadership. You can't come up with the idea and simply give it to your quality assurance person, who will give it to a consultant, while you hope that the program will be instigated.

Even after you attain ISO 9000 certification, your journey isn't over. Quality and ISO 9000 certification means a commitment to *continuous* improvement. Throw out the old saying, "If it ain't broke don't fix it." Once you go with a quality program like ISO 9000, your new saying will be, "If it ain't broke, let's see if we can make it better!"

Robert Caine, president of the American Society for Quality Control (ASQC) says, "For ISO to work, it has to go beyond the reports of hired quality consultants or internal quality professionals. People throughout the organization must be aware of the standards. People in production, purchasing, documentation, out in the field, people in post-production work, all have to come to terms with standards, get ownership of them, be involved in the whole process."

Caine's statement really underlies the importance of training, training necessary for people to do their job and training to understand what ISO 9000 is all about—for everybody in the organization.

It Takes Documentation and More

Registration under ISO 9000 is almost all about your policies and procedures. Is what you say you're doing what you're really doing? ISO 9000 series quality standards will force you to document what is supposed to happen, how it is supposed to be done, who is supposed to do it, where is it to occur, and when it is to occur.

For instance, if your company wants registration under the most comprehensive standard, ISO 9001, you must document everything from how you prepare design documents and maintain equipment to how you train employees and provide customer service.

WHAT DOES IT TAKE? (continued)

Although you may be initially put off by the amount of documentation ISO 9000 requires, rest easier . . . you may have much of it done already! Your documentation of processes, work instructions, testing procedures, and the like may be scattered all over your facility. Maybe it's written down and filed away, or perhaps some of it is in somebody's head. ISO 9000 will discipline you to create a verifiable, trackable, written-down, easily retrieved filing system. It's like the difference between having a handwritten, messy manual filing system versus the speed, structure, and efficiency of having everything on computer disks sorted by a sophisticated database.

John H. Switzer, writing in Xerox Engineering Systems Digest, says your ISO 9000 documentation system should contain several elements:

1. You should have a quality policy, a formal statement of mission that gives direction to your company and employees. It can be as simple as "customers come first."

2. You should have a quality manual that provides general assignment of and guidance for the authorities and responsibilities of the various departments. It describes how your company operates. You don't need to change these two documents unless your mission or company changes.

3. You need to document your operating procedures. This provides the details for the operation of a specific activity within your company. It assigns authority and responsibility within a department and describes how the work is done. For instance, procedures for all normal activities in a receiving department or an inspection department would be discussed here. These procedures may provide explicit instructions to employees on how to perform a task.

4. Most of these procedures and work instructions will generate records. This is the lowest level of documentation. Such records might include inspection reports, audit reports, completed purchase orders, and shipping requests. These records are evidence of the effectiveness of your quality system. You must carefully control and maintain them. You must catalog and control all of this documentation during its life cycle—from initial issue, to revision, to storage, to the trash can.

To be certified in an ISO 9000 series standard, you must have your quality system audited by a registered independent third-party auditor called a registrar. But you must also have in place an internal auditing system to provide for routine checks of all quality activities to make sure the quality system is working. Your audit team will issue a report to the audited area with a request for corrective action, if necessary. When corrective action is requested, the audit team will reaudit the department to make sure the problem has been corrected.

WHAT ARE THE BENEFITS OF CERTIFICATION?

The worst reason to comply with ISO 9000 is because you have to. You'll never get the full benefits, and there are many.

An ISO quality system is necessary because you don't do business in a static (nonchanging) environment. You already know that if you are in business. If you stay the same, your customers will change. And your competitors, the smart ones at least, will change to meet your customers' new needs.

In addition to allowing you the chance to "clean up your act" by going through a system that makes you examine your organization, its practices and methods, and find out where your strengths and weaknesses lie, here are some added benefits:

- **Gain worldwide recognition as a supplier of high-quality goods or services.** This is something most ISO 9000 series certificate-holders use to gain a marketing advantage over their competitors. It's a chance to tell your local, state, and association publications your story.

- **Reduce rework, inspections, warranty work, repairs, scrap, and other inefficiencies, thereby reducing operating costs.** The U.S. government estimates between 20% and 30% of the U.S. gross national product is wasted yearly on these inefficiencies. The savings per employee per year by reducing rework and the like can be $5,100 for a $10-an-hour employee. A 1991 General Accounting Office study showed companies that had a quality management system like ISO 9000 in place could expect to see improvements in product reliability of 11.3%, improvements in on-time deliveries of 4.7%, improvements in inventory turnovers of 7.2%, decreases in customer complaints of 11.6%, increases in market share of 13.7%, and increases in sales per employee of 8.6%.

- **Reduce the costs of stress.** By effectively implementing ISO 9000, you empower employees by assuring that they have the necessary tools and training to do the best job. This, according to Alex Dely in *Manufacturing News,* will reduce workplace stress. Using a conservative estimate, avoiding one stress-related workers' compensation claim per five-year period can cut costs by $3,000 per employee. A 25% reduction in doctor visits can also result in medical-cost savings of $250 per employee per year. A 10% decrease in stress-caused absenteeism can generate a savings of at least $160 per employee per year.

COSTS VERSUS BENEFITS

In a recent survey of 1,700 ISO 9000-registered firms in the U.S. and Canada, Deloitte & Touche conducted and reported in *Quality Systems Update* the following statistics relating to the costs versus benefits of implementing ISO:

- Companies *paid* $245,000 on average for costs associated with registration, including auditing fees and internal expenses. Remember, the costs are much lower for companies that have some form of quality system in place. These companies recoup that initial cost of registration on average in three years.

- Companies *saved* an average of $179,000 annually after registration (companies with average annual sales of $11 million or less reported an annual savings of $25,000; companies with annual sales of $1 billion reported an average savings per year of $532,000!).

- Eighty percent of the registered companies say ISO 9000 registration influences their choice of suppliers.

- Almost 83% of the registered companies say they encourage some suppliers to seek registration and 34% encourage all suppliers to seek registration.

- More than 80% of the registered companies say they use ISO 9000 registration as a criterion for selecting suppliers.

SELLING YOUR EMPLOYEES ON ISO 9000

Once you decide ISO 9000 is for you and you have convinced all of your company's leadership to expend the energy and money needed to make it happen, you should also take the time to sell it to your employees. With everybody's hearts, minds, and bodies in your quest for ISO 9000 series certification, you will end up spending less and making it happen more quickly.

Roger Landrum reported several key selling points in a recent article in *Quality Digest*. Here are seven points you can use to convince employees ISO 9000 is good for them, too:

> ► *ISO 9000 standards are common sense on paper.* Say what you do and do what you say.

> ► *ISO 9000 means job stability.* No longer are employees at the whim of changeable or moody bosses. ISO job procedures can be amended, but only through group consensus.

> ► *ISO 9000 certification requires employee input to write practical, user-friendly procedures.* Management must not write the procedures alone; it has to be done with input from everybody in the process.

> ► *ISO 9000 certification improves union relations.* The series defines and standardizes jobs. Employees are less at the whim of individual managers and more involved in group decision making about procedures and processes.

> ► *ISO 9000 will give your company a consistency of purpose.*

> ► *ISO 9000 provides for standard training tools and user-friendly guides and manuals.*

> ► *ISO 9000 makes you focus on what your customer wants.*

HOW TO CONVINCE THE BOSS

Knowing what you know about ISO 9000 series quality standards, you think it is a good idea that your company pursue certification. But your boss is a "bottom line" person. Try the following exercises to convince him or her:

▶ In a few sentences, how would you describe ISO 9000?

1. _____

_____

2. _____

_____

3. _____

_____

▶ Given what you know about your business and your boss, what arguments (in order of importance) would you use to get the *boss* to say "yes" to an ISO 9000 certification program? Be specific and concrete.

1. _____

_____

2. _____

_____

3. _____

_____

▶ You also know your boss might have some concerns that *employees* wouldn't support an ISO 9000 quality movement. What arguments could you use to convince the employees of your company?

1. _____

_____

2. _____

_____

3. _____

_____

CONCLUSION

ISO 9000 certification is a worldwide quality systems standard that will make your company more competitive at home and allow you to enter and compete in foreign markets. Even if you are not obligated to become ISO 9000 certified, there are tremendous benefits in doing so, such as being more productive and having greater employee and customer satisfaction.

Unfortunately, many North American companies will wait until their industrial governing body or target market mandates certification. By then, it may be too late to save some contracts.

What is your reason for *not* getting ISO 9000 certification?

SECTION

II

The ISO Family
of Standards

"Excellence is not an act,
but a habit."

—Aristotle

WHAT IS ISO MADE UP OF?

The ISO standard is comprised of five basic documents: ISO 9000 through ISO 9004. Your company would apply for certification under the part that most closely fits your form of business.

ISO 9000 to 9003

ISO 9000 is actually a series of guidelines for selection and use of the appropriate systems standards of **ISO 9001, ISO 9002,** or **ISO 9003.** *ISO 9000 News* calls ISO 9000 the roadmap to the entire series. ISO 9000 presents guidance on the selection and use of quality management and assurance standards by explaining what the entire series is all about, for both supplier and customer. ISO 9000 goes into detail on the general philosophy of the quality systems standards, their characteristics, the existing types, where and when you can best use them, and what elements quality assurance models should incorporate. It also covers demonstration and documentation requirements, precontract assessment, and contract preparation.

ISO 9004

Skipping ahead to **ISO 9004,** it has been called the set of building blocks that make it possible to customize quality standards and make them conform to real-life situations in your business. ISO 9004 is the basic element in the process of building up a quality system that you can fit to your specific situation.

For instance, a construction company has decided to put in place an ISO 9000 quality system. The designated team looks through all 20 elements in ISO 9004 (covered later) and decides the ones it will keep and the ones it can do without. Not every company will use the same 20 quality items because requirements or production processes are not the same from one company or industry to another. But there is a minimal list of topics that must be part of any system deserving a quality label. The company must make sure it takes everything it needs to put in its own quality-management specifications. Another construction company will probably come up with the same choices. However, a machine tool company would come up with a different list. So would a law firm, and so on. The point is, the quality elements you choose depend on your business; they are not forced on you.

WHAT IS ISO MADE UP OF? (continued)

The topics in ISO 9004 cover 20 detailed chapters. They are risk, cost and benefits, management responsibility, quality-system principles, system documentation and auditing, economics, quality in marketing, quality in specification and design, in procurement, quality in production, control of production, product verification, control of measuring and test equipment, nonconformity, corrective action, handling and post-production action, quality documentation and records, personnel, product safety and liability, training, and statistical methods.

Once you customize an ISO 9000 series management and quality-assurance system for your business, a customer or an independent body, such as a registrar, can assess you (necessary if you want official certification). The most important thing an assessor will look at is that you have covered the basic quality elements that pertain to your business, industry, and customers.

Your location actually gets certified to either ISO 9001, ISO 9002, or ISO 9003.

THE ISO 9000 SERIES: FROM 9001 TO 9003

What Is ISO 9001?

ISO 9001 is the most comprehensive part of ISO. It applies to facilities that design, develop, produce, install, and service products or services to customers who specify how the product or service is to perform. ISO 9001 consists of all 20 quality elements. It is most typically used by manufacturing organizations that design their own products and build them.

What Is ISO 9002?

ISO 9002 applies to facilities that provide goods or services consistent with designs or specifications furnished by the customer. In past years, says Gary Spizizen,* process industries such as chemical and paint manufacturing relied on ISO 9002 exclusively. However, more and more of these industries are starting to understand how their new product research and development processes fit the definition of "design" under ISO—and they are opting more for the ISO 9001 standard. ISO 9002 consists of 18 parts (out of the 20 that are in ISO 9001) and deals with internal quality audits, corrective action, process control, purchaser supplier product control, purchasing, and contract review.

What Is ISO 9003?

ISO 9003 applies to final inspection and test procedures only and is the least detailed of the ISO 9000 family of standards. It requires that you assure only conformance in final test and inspection. Of the three core standards (ISO 9001, ISO 9002, and ISO 9003), this one has the least marketing value and is the least often applied for. It is usually used by organizations such as testing laboratories, calibration houses, and equipment distributors that inspect and test supplied products. It consists of 12 of the 20 parts required in ISO 9001.

---

*Spizizen, Gary, "The ISO 9000 Standards: Creating a Level of Playing Field for International Quality," *National Productivity Review*, Summer 1992, pp. 331–345.

The ISO 9000 Series from Top to Bottom

ISO 9000
Guidelines for Selection and Use
"The Roadmap to the System"

ISO 9004
Guidelines on Quality System Requirements (internal
quality management purpose, system design)
"The Building Blocks"

ISO 9001
Quality in Design, Development, Production,
Installation, and Services
"The Most Comprehensive"

or

ISO 9002
Quality in Production and Installation
"Covers 18 of 20 Elements"

or

ISO 9003
Quality in Final Inspection and Testing
"The Least Comprehensive"

A caution: seek expert advice in picking the right standard. Getting certified to the least comprehensive series, ISO 9003, will be worthless and a waste of your time and money if your customers want your quality assurance at the ISO 9001 level.

WHICH ISO STANDARD TO CHOOSE?

What ISO standard should you attempt to certify your facility in? ISO 9001? ISO 9002? ISO 9003? It depends on your business and what you do, and what your customer may want you certified in.

What does your facility do? Do you:

1. Design, develop, produce, install, and service your product or service?

   If YES, *pick ISO 9001, the most comprehensive standard. If* NO, *go to question 2.*

2. Do you manufacture products to specifications given to you by outside contractors? Do you need to conform to specified production and installation requirements.

   If YES, *pick ISO 9002, containing 18 of the 20 elements of ISO 9001. If* NO, *go to question 3.*

3. Are you a testing laboratory, calibration house, or equipment distributor that inspects and tests supplied products? Do you need to assure quality only in final test and inspection?

   If YES, *pick ISO 9003, containing 12 of the 20 elements of ISO 9001, and the least comprehensive of the series. If you again answered* NO, *consult expert opinion such as consultants and trade associations in your industry. Find out what ISO series other similar companies are certifying under.*

CONCLUSION

ISO 9000 is really a series of standards. You'll either get certified in the most stringent area, ISO 9001; ISO 9002; or the least stringent area, ISO 9003. Which ISO 9000 series you choose depends on you, your industry, and what series your customers want you to get certified in.

SECTION

III

The Twenty Elements of ISO 9000 Series Quality

"Quality is not any single thing, but an aura, an atmosphere, an overpowering feeling that a company is doing everything with excellence."

—John F. Welch, CEO, General Electric

THE TWENTY ELEMENTS

The following 20 elements and explanations comprise the ISO 9000 series standard. All elements apply to ISO 9001, 18 of the elements apply to ISO 9002, and 12 of the elements apply to ISO 9003.

A registrar will assess whether or not your facility meets the particular ISO series elements based on documentation and performance. An approved third-party registrar will certify your facility by reviewing your quality manual to see you meet the particular ISO 9000 series standard and by auditing your processes to make sure the system you document in your manual is actually what you are doing.

It is perhaps easiest to understand what the 20 elements of ISO 9000 ask you to do by posing questions. (See Section V for a more in-depth interpretation of all 20 elements.)

QUALITY SYSTEM REQUIREMENTS

4.1 Management Responsibility

Who is responsible for making sure the product is what the customer ordered? Who ensures you effectively manage your quality system?

Note: ISO 9001 (4.1) is less stringent in ISO 9002 (4.1) and even less stringent in ISO 9003 (4.1).

4.1.1 Quality Policy: Have you defined and documented your quailty policy to meet the minimum requirements of ISO 9000?

4.1.2 Organization: Is your quality approach effective? Does it define who is responsible for what? Do you have a way to address problems systematically and solve them by getting at the root cause?

> **4.1.2.1 Responsibility and authority:** Do you have someone responsible for quality? Have you given this person the authority and freedom to seek out and fix quality problems?

> **4.1.2.2 Resources:** Do you have an in-house auditing system? Are your auditors adequately trained?

> **4.1.2.3 Management representative:** Do you have a management representative to keep track of all the requirements and documents for ISO 9000?

4.1.3 Management Review: Do your senior managers regularly review the results of the quality system audit? Do you make sure you use the results to make any necessary changes?

4.2 Quality System

Is your quality system in place to make sure you deliver everything to the customer that you promised? How do you make sure?

Note: ISO 9001 (4.2) is less stringent in ISO 9003 (4.2).

4.2.1 General: Do you maintain a quality manual?

4.2.2 Quality System Procedures: Are your documented procedures consistent with ISO 9000?

4.2.3 Quality Planning: Do you define and document how you will meet the requirements for quality?

4.3 Contract Review

What system do you use to assure the customer that what you or your marketing and sales staff promised the customer is what is delivered and on time?

Note: ISO 9001 (4.3) does not apply to ISO 9003.

4.3.1 General: Do you have procedures for contract review? How do you coordinate these procedures?

4.3.2 Review: What system do you use to make sure contracts and orders are defined and documented? How do you correct any problems with contracts? How do you make sure you can fulfill the contract for the customer?

4.3.3 Amendment to Contract: How do you amend contracts? How do you make sure everybody who needs to know about the changes actually finds out?

4.3.4 Records: How do you maintain records of contract reviews?

4.4 Design Control

How did you design your product or service? How do you know it does what you say it does? Do your designers and salespeople agree that it works as you say? If you make document changes, how do you make sure the product or service is still good?

Note: ISO 9001 (4.4) does not apply to ISO 9002 or ISO 9003.

4.4.1 General: Do you maintain a documented process for product design that does what you promised your customers?

4.4.2 Design and Development Planning: Do you define how the design process is done? Who is involved? How do they communicate? What paths do the processes take? Is the design process under regular management review?

4.4.3 Organizational and Technical Interfaces: What people and departments come into the design process?

QUALITY SYSTEM REQUIREMENTS
(continued)

4.4.4 Design Input: What system do you use to ensure the design group receives all design requirements?

4.4.5 Design Review: What kinds of formal design reviews do you conduct? How do you maintain records of these reviews?

4.4.6 Design Output: Do you document and maintain design output such as drawings, test requirements, tolerance requirements, assembly instructions, and test methodologies? Have you adequately referenced any regulatory or association standards or critical requirements to the design?

4.4.7 Design Verification: Do you conduct formal and documented reviews of the product design? Are the reviewers independent of the design function?

4.4.8 Design Validation: How do you make sure design conforms to user needs or requirements?

4.4.9 Design Changes: What system do you use to make and control design changes?

4.5. Document Control

How do you let manufacturing employees know of the requirements and materials they'll need to build the customers' product or service? If you make any change to the requirements, how do you let the appropriate people know? If a customer needs parts, can you tell him or her what to order? If you make changes in material requirements, how do you let manufacturing know? Will your service people know what parts to use for repairs?

> *Note: ISO 9001 (4.5) is the same as ISO 9002 (4.4) and ISO 9003 (4.3). This is a less stringent element in ISO 9003.*

4.5.1 General: Do you have a procedure to control all documents and data that relate to the ISO 9000 series requirement?

4.5.2 Document Approval and Issue: Do you have a formal document-control system? Are documents easily obtained? Do you remove outdated material?

4.5.3 Document Changes: How do you oversee document changes?

4.6 Purchasing

Can you prove how you make sure your purchasing people buy what your engineers and designers ask for? How do you assure you're buying a good-quality product from your suppliers? Do the suppliers deliver on time?

Note: ISO 9001 (4.6) does not apply to ISO 9003. ISO 9001 (4.6) is the same as ISO 9002 (4.5).

4.6.1 General: How do you assure your purchasing department gets the right materials for any specified requirements?

4.6.2 Evaluation of Subcontractors: What formal review system do you use to evaluate subcontractors? How and where do you maintain these records?

4.6.3 Purchasing Data: How do you identify the material you purchase? Do you make sure any purchase document contains notation of compliance to a standard like ISO 9000?

4.6.4 Verification of Purchased Product: Do you inspect the source of the product you've purchased?

4.6.4.1 Supplier verification at subcontractors: If you do check the purchased product on the subcontractor's premises, is this noted in the purchasing document?

4.6.4.2 Customer verification of subcontracted product: If it is specified in the contract, do you know you can verify that the purchased product conforms to specifications at the subcontractor's place of business?

4.7 Purchaser-Supplied Product

How do you store, protect, and maintain your materials? How do you fix problems you find with materials?

Note: ISO 9001 (4.7) does not apply to ISO 9003. ISO 9001 (4.7) is the same as ISO 9002 (4.6).

QUALITY SYSTEM REQUIREMENTS
(continued)

4.8 Product Identification and Traceability

How do you make sure your materials don't get mixed up with others? How do you assure those materials are what were ordered? How do you check the materials are what the drawings say they are? How do you make sure you use the right materials to make the customers' product?

> *Note: ISO 9001 (4.8) is the same as ISO 9002 (4.7) and ISO 9003 (4.4), but less stringent in ISO 9003.*

4.9 Process Control

Can you prove your procedures are in place to build the customers' product correctly? Do you know when you're making a bad product? Are there points in your process where you can't tell by inspection if the product is correct? How do you handle this? Are procedures written down so your people can easily get them or use them to train others?

> *Note: ISO 9001 (4.9) does not apply to ISO 9003. ISO 9001 (4.9) is the same as ISO 9002 (4.8).*

4.10 Inspection and Testing

How do you make sure the customer gets what he or she ordered? How do you know what the customer ordered actually works? Can you show the customer how you tested the workability of the product?

> *Note: ISO 9001 (4.10) is the same as ISO 9002 (4.9) and ISO 9003 (4.5) but not as stringent in ISO 9003.*

4.10.1 General: Do you have and maintain documented procedures for inspection and testing?

4.10.2 Receiving Inspection and Testing: What system do you use to ensure that incoming product isn't used until it has been inspected? Where do you store an incoming product that fails inspection?

4.10.3 In-Process Inspection and Testing: How do you document your in-process inspection and testing procedures?

4.10.4 Final Inspection and Testing: How do you test and inspect your final product? How do you maintain records to document that your product meets your testing requirements and the tests were conducted following your quality plan?

4.10.5 Final Inspection and Test Records: Do you maintain records which prove you inspected and/or tested the product? What do you do with any non-passing product? Do your records show who is responsible for approving the release of any product?

4.11 Inspection, Measuring, and Test Equipment

How do you make sure your test equipment is accurate?

> *Note: ISO 9001 (4.11) is the same as ISO 9002 (4.10) and ISO 9003 (4.6), but not as stringent in ISO 9003.*

4.11.1 General: Have you established and maintained documented procedures to control, calibrate, and maintain inspection, measuring, and test equipment?

4.11.2 Control Procedure: How do you make sure you measure what you're supposed to measure with equipment that is workable and accurate?

4.12 Inspection and Test Status

How do you show on the product or service that you tested it?

> *Note: ISO 9001 (4.12) is the same as ISO 9002 (4.11) and ISO 9003 (4.7), but not as stringent in ISO 9003.*

QUALITY SYSTEM REQUIREMENTS
(continued)

4.13 Control of Nonconforming Product

What procedure do you use to fix a customer's broken product? Do all your people know what to do when they fix the product? How do you retest a fixed product? How do you make sure a broken product isn't mixed in with other products?

> *Note: ISO 9001 (4.13) is the same as ISO 9002 (4.12) and ISO 9003 (4.8), but not as stringent in ISO 9003.*

4.13.1 General: How do you make sure a bad product isn't accidentally used? How do you separate bad product from good product?

4.13.2 Nonconforming Product Review and Disposition: Who has the responsibility to review, and authority to dispose of, a bad product?

4.14 Corrective Action

What procedure do you follow when you find a problem in a product? Do you write new procedures or train people to make sure the problem doesn't happen again?

> *Note: ISO 9001 (4.14) does not apply to ISO 9003. ISO 9001 (4.14) is the same as ISO 9002 (4.13).*

4.14.1 General: What kind of documented procedure do you follow to implement corrective and preventive actions?

4.14.2 Corrective Action: How do you handle customer complaints? How do you investigate the cause of problems? How do you determine what corrective action needs to be done to eliminate the root cause of the problem? What controls do you have to make sure corrective action is taken and is effective?

4.14.3 Preventive Action: What procedures do you follow to prevent problems?

4.15 Handling, Storage, Packaging, and Delivery

How do you assure the customer that his or her product was built correctly? How do you make sure you package and store the product to prevent damage? How can you assure the customer the product won't be damaged in delivery?

Note: ISO 9001 (4.15) is the same as ISO 9002 (4.14) and ISO 9003 (4.9), but not as stringent in ISO 9003.

4.15.1 General: What documented procedures do you follow to handle, store, package, preserve, and deliver your product?

4.15.2 Handling: How do you handle a product to make sure it isn't damaged or destroyed?

4.15.3 Storage: Do you store products or materials to prevent damage?

4.15.4 Packaging: Do you document your methods of properly packaging materials?

4.15.5 Preservation: Do you use appropriate methods to preserve and segregate the product?

4.15.6 Delivery: Is the product delivered in accordance to the contract?

4.16 Quality Records

What procedures do you follow to document the quality of your product or service? Could you produce these records quickly if the customer wanted to see them?

Note: ISO 9001 (4.16) is the same as ISO 9002 (4.15) and ISO 9003 (4.10), but not as stringent in ISO 9003.

QUALITY SYSTEM REQUIREMENTS (continued)

4.17 Internal Quality Audits

How can you prove you're running your company as you say you do? Have you trained a group of your people to review your organization regularly? Can you produce records to show you've given attention to critical areas in your operation? Can you prove where management has corrected a problem an audit team has pointed out?

> *Note: ISO 9001 (4.17) does not apply to ISO 9003. ISO 9001 (4.17) is ISO 9002 (4.16), but not as stringent in ISO 9002.*

4.18 Training

Can you prove the people who made and tested the customers' product or service were properly trained?

> *Note: ISO 9001 (4.18) is the same as ISO 9002 (4.17), but ISO 9002 (4.17) is less stringent. ISO 9003 (4.11) is the same as ISO 9001 (4.18), but less stringent than ISO 9002 (4.17).*

4.19 Servicing

How would you service the customers' product? Can you ensure that your servicing operation will make the customer satisfied? How do you make sure the customers' product is serviced by trained personnel?

> *Note: ISO 9001 (4.19) does not apply to ISO 9002 or ISO 9003.*

4.20 Statistical Techniques

If you use statistical techniques to assure product quality, can you show how the techniques work? Does everybody know what to do if the statistics show a process is out of control or outside the control limits?

4.20.1 Identification of Need: How do you identify what statistical technique is required to establish, verify, and control process capability and product characteristics?

4.20.2 Procedures: What system do you use to make sure you're using the right statistical measures?

> *Note: ISO 9001 (4.20) is the same as ISO 9002 (4.18) and ISO 9003 (4.12), but less stringent in ISO 9003.*

ISO 9000 SERIES COMPLIANCE CHECKLIST

What ISO series do you want certification for? ISO 9001? ISO 9002? ISO 9003? Use the following checklist as a guide to see how well you're doing.

ISO 9001 Section #	Section Description	OK	NI	NC	NA
4.1	Management Responsibility	☐	☐	☐	☐
4.1.1	Quality Policy	☐	☐	☐	☐
4.1.2	Organization	☐	☐	☐	☐
4.1.2.1	Responsibility and Authority	☐	☐	☐	☐
4.1.2.2	Verification of Resources and Personnel	☐	☐	☐	☐
4.1.2.3	Management Representative	☐	☐	☐	☐
4.1.3	Management Review	☐	☐	☐	☐
4.2	Quality System	☐	☐	☐	☐
4.3	Contract Review	☐	☐	☐	☐
4.4	Design Control	☐	☐	☐	☐
4.4.2	Design and Development Planning	☐	☐	☐	☐
4.4.2.1	Design Activity Assignment	☐	☐	☐	☐
4.4.2.2	Design Organizational and Technical Interfaces	☐	☐	☐	☐

Key:

OK = You are in compliance with this element or part of element.
NI = You need to improve in this area.
NC = You are not in compliance in this area.
NA = This element does not apply to your facility.

ISO 9001 Section #	Section Description	OK	NI	NC	NA
4.4.6	Design Output	☐	☐	☐	☐
4.4.7	Design Verification	☐	☐	☐	☐
4.4.9	Design Changes	☐	☐	☐	☐
4.5.2	Document Approval and Issue	☐	☐	☐	☐
4.6	Purchasing	☐	☐	☐	☐
4.6.2	Evaluation of Subcontractors	☐	☐	☐	☐
4.6.3	Purchasing Data	☐	☐	☐	☐
4.6.4	Verification of Purchased Product	☐	☐	☐	☐
4.7	Purchaser-Supplied Product	☐	☐	☐	☐
4.8	Product Identification and Traceability	☐	☐	☐	☐
4.9	Process Control	☐	☐	☐	☐
4.9.2	Special Processes	☐	☐	☐	☐
4.10.2	Receiving Inspection and Testing	☐	☐	☐	☐
4.10.3	In-Process Inspection and Testing	☐	☐	☐	☐
4.10.4	Final Inspection and Testing	☐	☐	☐	☐
4.10.5	Final Inspection and Test Records	☐	☐	☐	☐
4.11	Inspection, Measuring, and Test Equipment	☐	☐	☐	☐
4.12	Inspection and Test Status	☐	☐	☐	☐

ISO 9000 SERIES COMPLIANCE CHECKLIST (continued)

ISO 9001 Section #	Section Description	OK	NI	NC	NA
4.13.2	Review and Disposition of Nonconforming Product	☐	☐	☐	☐
4.14	Corrective Action	☐	☐	☐	☐
4.15	Handling, Storage, Packaging, and Delivery	☐	☐	☐	☐
4.15.2	Handling	☐	☐	☐	☐
4.15.3	Storage	☐	☐	☐	☐
4.15.4	Packaging	☐	☐	☐	☐
4.15.6	Delivery	☐	☐	☐	☐
4.16	Quality Records	☐	☐	☐	☐
4.17	Internal Quality Audits	☐	☐	☐	☐
4.18	Training	☐	☐	☐	☐
4.19	Servicing	☐	☐	☐	☐
4.20	Statistical Techniques	☐	☐	☐	☐

CONCLUSION

The 20 elements in ISO 9001 (18 apply to ISO 9002 and 12 apply to ISO 9003) will allow you and your employees to ask fundamental questions about how you do business. Asking the questions is the first step toward continuous process improvement.

How you apply and interpret the standards is, again, something you must customize for your business. The items are intentionally written generally; *you* have to supply the specifics!

IV

On the Road to Certification

"It does not matter how slowly you go as long as you do not stop."

—Confucius

A CAUTIONARY NOTE

As you probably have guessed by now, certification to one of the ISO 9000 series standards takes documentation. But some companies, in the zealous attempt to impress ISO 9000 auditors, *over*document.

Case Study: More Isn't Always Better

David Kenney, director of quality at ADC Kentrox, described how his firm's first attempt at ISO documentation almost destroyed the company.

Kenney told the *Wall Street Journal* it first produced a 100-plus-page document that described in "excruciating detail" the activities needed to bring a product from first concept through first shipment to the customer. The initial report required project managers to track, verify, and document more than 50 items across eight phases of the product introduction process.

A company manager told ADC Kentrox, "We didn't follow your new product introduction process because if we had, the project would have been delayed by months. If we had twice the people, we still couldn't have followed this monstrosity."

Their ISO team withdrew the documentation and studied what it did wrong.

Case Study Review

We can learn from these mistakes:

1. ADC Kentrox had not included the right people in the design of the procedures. It needed more involvement from engineering and manufacturing people, and less from corporate managers.

2. ADC Kentrox had not fully studied its unique situation. It is a small, market-leading company with 250 employees. It decided it needed to be flexible, easy, and quick to implement procedures, the opposite of the approach it had originally taken in its attempt to please ISO auditors. Often, people will create unneeded documentation, thinking the ISO auditors grade their ISO 9000 quality system on the weight of their manual! No . . . content matters. Remember, you must prove to the auditors you do what you say you do.

A CAUTIONARY NOTE (continued)

3. ADC Kentrox then restructured its new product introduction
process to include a decentralization of responsibilities and a flexible
approach to project management. It reduced its total documentation
by half. ADC Kentrox found that if it documented company decisions,
it had no problem complying with ISO 9001 (and its 20 elements)
requirements.

The result? In 1993, ADC Kentrox became one of the first companies in the
telecommunications equipment industry to earn ISO 9001 certification.

HOW LONG DOES CERTIFICATION TAKE?

The amount of time it takes you to certify to one of the ISO 9000 standards depends on the current state of your quality system and documentation:

- If your company uses a quality system framework such as Category 5 of the Baldrige criteria (*Management of Process Quality*) or MIL-Q-9858A, you may reach ISO 9000 series conformance in **less than 12 months** with a minimum of consulting help.

- If your company has sketchy procedures or is relatively unsophisticated in the application of quality methods and procedures, you might reach ISO 9000 series conformance **from 12 to 15 months.**

- If your company is starting a quality system from scratch and you have less than a full commitment from your senior leadership, it will take you **up to and beyond 24 months** to reach ISO 9000-level quality.

Another note of caution: Research on certification shows an initial ISO 9000 series failure rate of about 60% for companies that try to prepare without outside consulting help. My advice is that the more sophisticated your company is on ISO 9000, the less need you have for outside help.

WHAT DOES CERTIFICATION COST?

First, think of an ISO 9000 series certificate of registration in terms of the benefits listed in Section I. The benefits you get depend on your industry and your particular business, but they can be sizable. Some facilities recoup the cost associated with ISO 9000 in as little as nine months.

Total costs do vary on the size of your plant and your industry, but here are some ballpark figures for a company of modest size:

- Total consulting fees, based on fees of $1,000 per day, might fall between $25,000 to $80,000.

- The fees to the registrar you select are $1,000 per day plus travel and expenses for a minimum of 10 days. At the very least, a registrar will bill you for one or two days for the initial visit, a two- to three-day preliminary audit, and a three- to five-day registration audit. Thus total registrar fees may range from $10,000 to $30,000.

- Your total cost (consulting and registrar) will range anywhere from $35,000 to $110,000-plus. The smaller the firm, normally the lower the total cost.

And remember, certification to an ISO 9000 series standard requires your firm undergo a surveillance audit about every six months and an entire re-audit every three years.

FOLLOW THESE STEPS TO ISO 9000 CERTIFICATION . . .

FOURTEEN STEPS TO CERTIFICATION

Depending on where your company is in its quality journey, the total time for certification will take anywhere from under 12 months to more than 24 months. Adjust your timeline accordingly.

Before you get started on the road to ISO 9000 series certification, it is absolutely mandatory you have senior-level leadership commitment. Not the kind of commitment that delegates this project to the quality person; what you need is hands-on, everyday concern from the top. Get a letter of support from senior leadership for the process. Make sure ISO 9000 is at the top of every staff meeting agenda. Repeat the leadership's commitment over and over again to everybody in your organization.

Once you have this kind of top-level support, you can follow this 14-step system to get ISO 9000 series certification.

STEP 1: Establish and Train an ISO 9000 Steering Council

Include representatives of all areas touched by ISO 9000 certification. And make sure these people are the best. You don't want this committee to fail the company. The supervisors must also understand the ISO 9000 steering council's representatives will need a certain amount of time off to devote to their assignments. In addition, you should appoint one person, a kind of ISO 9000 "guru," to be the main person to interact with consultants and the registrar. Train the ISO council to understand all aspects of ISO 9000 requirements thoroughly. These trained council members become roving experts who can spread the word about ISO 9000 and answer people's questions.

Specific actions the council needs to take include:

- Review the existing quality manual (if it exists).

- Select what ISO 9000 series your company will eventually attempt certification for (either 9001, the most comprehensive; 9002, or 9003).

- Identify any industry or military standards you can integrate with ISO 9000.

- Develop a consensus on what ISO 9000 is within your organization.

FOURTEEN STEPS TO CERTIFICATION (continued)

STEP 2: Evaluate and Select a Registrar

This may be one of the most important steps in getting ISO 9000 certification. Think of selecting your registrar much like selecting a mate for marriage. Not just anyone will be best for you. Get information and costs from a variety of registrars. Interview the ones you think are the best fit for your company and industry. Do not wait to meet your registrar for the first time at your certification audit.

A quality systems registrar will evaluate your quality system for conformity to ISO 9001, ISO 9002, or ISO 9003. If your quality system conforms, the registrar issues you a certificate. The certification is then listed in a register that is available to the public. You can then mention or display the registrar's approval on advertising and your stationery as evidence of registration.

Here are some questions to ask a potential registrar:

- *Does the registrar specialize in your particular industry?*

- *Is the registrar recognized in the target country or countries you plan to export to? Do they have MOU's (memoranda of understanding) with other registration organizations that mutually recognize each other's certification?*

- *What references can the registrar furnish you?* Check them!

- *What are the registrar's costs?* Try to get information on application fees, initial visit costs, the certification audit costs, costs of future meetings, and cancellation fees.

- *Is the registrar available to you when you call?* Or do you get the run-around.

- *Does the registrar have an office near your facility?* This can save you money on travel expenses.

- *How does the registrar evaluate your quality system?* Some give pass/fail grades; others give you a score.

- *What happens if you don't pass the quality audit?* Some registrars will re-audit in 30 days and look only at the areas in which you needed improvement; others will make you start again from ground zero. Make sure you cover in the contract you sign how yours will handle any follow-ups.

- *Does the registrar have confidentiality agreements with its employees and all who might see your audit results?*

- *Can you meet the lead auditor?* Does he or she understand your industry? Try to understand what the lead auditor's expectations are. This will help in planning for the audit.

- *What are the qualifications of the lead auditor and auditors the registrar uses?* In the United States, many auditors and lead auditors are trained in accordance with the American Society for Quality Control's Certified Quality Auditor (CQA) standards.

- *How can you tell people if your company passes the registrar's certification audit?* How can you inform your customers? Normally, you're placed in a registry where customers and competitors can look you up. Announcement of your certification should also appear in *Quality Systems Update.*

STEP 3: Determine Who Is Responsible for Quality

Involve everybody from the president on down who is responsible for quality. You need to document that there is an actual activity associated with every defined responsibility. Your steering council should identify every area of your company that will be affected by the ISO 9000 standard.

Obtain or create an organizational chart showing how quality responsibility flows in your company. This will make the auditing job easier.

FOURTEEN STEPS TO CERTIFICATION (continued)

STEP 4: Determine How to Structure Your Procedures

How will you format your procedures? How can you maintain this structure?

One strategy uses two or three layers of procedures. The few stable procedures go at the top of the structure; the great number of variable procedures goes lower.

At the top are corporate-level procedures that focus on the various standards you suppport, how to approach ISO 9000 requirements, and how you define the corporate quality assurance responsibility. Be brief.

The second level would cover plant or group-level procedures. They define practices that are issued from the corporate level.

The third level is departmental operations where detailed procedures, records, and documents are maintained.

Think of the quality manual as being at the top of a pyramid. Your department procedures are at the second level and the detailed work instructions are at the bottom of the pyramid.

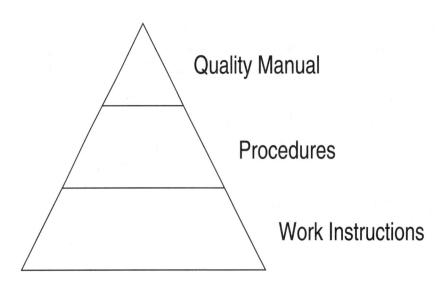

Quality Manual

Procedures

Work Instructions

The upper part of the pyramid, the quality manual, is available to customers and suppliers and contains little detailed technical and operational information.

Detailed procedures and work instructions, the second and third levels of the pyramid, are things you can store and maintain throughout your organization, close to the work and easy to retrieve.

It's a good idea to keep a unified numbering system throughout the three layers of documentation so you can track related documents upward and downward in the pyramid. This will make it easier to keep your entire pyramid of documentation up-to-date.

STEP 5: Let Individual Departments Develop Their Own Quality Manuals

The steering council should give each department, and its departmental quality coordinator, the basic requirements of the procedures. Let the individual departments have some freedom in documenting how each solves problems and ensures quality using maximum employee input.

There are three advantages of using this system to document your procedures:

- Since the document is internally produced, management input is high.

- The document addresses department needs instead of something that imposes an external requirement.

- Since insiders "in the know" produce the documents, there are fewer errors and omissions.

FOURTEEN STEPS TO CERTIFICATION (continued)

STEP 6: Define Document Standards

You and your ISO steering council are responsible for a number of documents and support records that will support the particular ISO 9000 standard you are working toward. Spread out the work among the quality team members at the lowest department level; these are the people who know and do the work best.

Here, with the help of Rabbitt and Bergh, is a list of documents, systems records, and contract/product records you must create:

I. Documentation	Pertaining to What ISO 9001 Element?
Quality Policy and Objectives	4.1.1
Quality Manual	4.2, note a
Design Control	4.4
Work Instructions	4.9.1
Final Inspections	4.10.3
Instrument Calibration	4.11.c
Nonconformities	4.13
Corrective Actions	4.14
Internal Quality Actions	4.17

II. Systems Records	Pertaining to What ISO 9001 Element?
Management Review	4.1.3
Subcontractors Assessment	4.6.2
Instrument Calibration	4.11.f
Audit Records	4.17
Training	4.18

III. Contract/Product Records	Pertaining to What ISO 9001 Element?
Contract Review	4.3
Design Verification	4.4.5.a
Product Identification	4.8
Inspection and Testing	4.10.4
Product Release	4.12
Nonconforming Product	4.13.1

STEP 7: Write the Quality Manual

Each department should develop its own individual procedures and detailed work instructions (using maximum employee input) following the structure developed by the steering council. Then the council must blend these documents into a facility-wide quality manual.

Preparation of the various parts of the documentation is best done by the people closest to the work. It's the job of your ISO 9000 steering council to make sure everybody follows a consistent structure, chapter by chapter (ISO element by ISO element), procedure by procedure, instruction by instruction.

This is important to do because the biggest single reason for audit failure is something registrars call *insufficient documentation.* Problems here include a lack of documentation on specific departmental procedures and/or training material and documents given to employees that they can't understand.

FOURTEEN STEPS TO CERTIFICATION (continued)

You should organize the final quality manual in an auditor-friendly way. Chapter by chapter, cover each of the 20 elements of ISO 9001 (or 18 elements of ISO 9002, or 12 elements of ISO 9003). The harder you make your manual to follow, the longer and harder the registrar's audit will be. Also note that the more you include in this document, the more the registrar has to audit! *More doesn't mean better.*

Once this manual gets steering council approval, you send it to the registrar you selected for document review. Some registrars perform a document review on-site; most perform the review at their own offices, saving you travel costs and expenses and the effort it would take you to host the registrar.

Remember to give yourself time to correct any problems the registrar might find in your quality manual.

STEP 8: Maintain Your Records and Documentation

Chapter 4, element 14 (4.16) of the ISO 9001 standard says certified companies must establish and maintain procedures for identification, collection, indexing, filing, storage, maintenance, disposition, and retrievability of quality records. What this means is you must have a system where you store records and documents of all kinds that is easy to access.

Some of the documents you'll need to control include:

- management review minutes
- quality manuals and plans
- assembly drawings
- customer specifications
- contracts
- standards used
- operating procedures
- work instructions

- lists of approved suppliers
- inspection records
- customer complaints
- product history and traceability
- internal audit reports
- personnel training files
- master lists of document revisions
- master document distribution lists

You must uniquely identify each of these documents with page, date, revision control signatures approved by authorized people, and the documents must be available to all designated workers.

Whew! Remember, documentation is a key element in getting certified to an ISO 9000 standard. If you don't take care in planning your system, you could easily drown yourself in documents and records.

There are two ways to maintain the records and documentation that are crucial to successful ISO 9000 certification: the traditional *paper-based* system successfully used by scores of certified facilities or a *computer-based* (RTNF or Real Time, Non Falsifiable) system.

The market is just starting to see some computer-based software that will make the job of maintaining records (ISO 9001 section 4.16) easier and will also give you the ability to trace what you put into your product and how you identify the product (ISO 9001 section 4.8). Future revisions of the ISO 9000 standards likely will expand traceability of your product to traceability of *all* decisions you make within your company.

A Word About RTNF

The enormous interest in RTNF computer-based systems is in part a result of efforts in the European Community and the United States regarding strict judgments in the area of product liability law. All a plaintiff needs to prove was that damage or injury was sustained as the result of using your product. Lack of ISO 9000 compliance is a plaintiff's easiest argument that you build a nonquality product. On the other hand, if you can trace and document every quality decision by every employee in a nonfalsifiable computer database (paper documents can be altered or falsified), you can defend yourself by saying you did everything possible. You might at least avoid punitive damages.

An RTNF system can also increase the reliability and speed of your decision-making system. This system can allow greater accuracy and faster invoicing and payment processing, possibly increasing cashflow. The computer-based system can make available key statistics on your company's performance, allowing greater efficiency, employee involvement, and teamwork.

FOURTEEN STEPS TO CERTIFICATION
(continued)

It will also allow immediate follow-up of customer complaints or inquiries. Your response can then be distributed to your customers, distributors, financial analysts, and media. It makes it possible to identify customer preferences and key customer-service issues. RTNF systems provide continuous updating of data—allowing you to advise customers on reliability, life expectancy, and special features of your product and service. It can provide continuous communication between your sales people and managers with your customers through electronic data interchange, allowing you to do market surveys almost immediately.

Finally, a fully implemented RTNF can provide you continuous and automatic inventory replenishment at the customer's location, which may be critical in just in time (JIT) production.

ISO 9000 puts a heavy emphasis on training, both widening and deepening the training and keeping records of training. Documentation of both on-the-job and classroom training of people is crucial since noncompliance in this area can shut your facility down. (For example, the U.S. Food and Drug Administration can stop your operation if you can't prove that all of your operators meet periodic retraining requirements.) An RTNF system can prove you regularly train key people involved in quality of your product or service.

Other benefits in using an RTNF system versus a traditional paper-based system include:

- *Ability to share data, records, and documents through computer local area networks*

- *Assuring all employees have the latest drawings, documentation, and procedures (with only authorized staff having access)*

- *Allowing use with other computer programs, such as statistical process control, relational databases, telecommunications, and so on . . . in addition to use with hardware such as programmable logic controls.*

The techology is new, but it holds great promise in reducing and controlling the paperwork explosion that comes from ISO 9000 certification.

You'll find a list of software (and other resources) for ISO 9000 at the end of this book.

STEP 9: Educate Everybody on ISO 9000

You need to let everybody in your organization know how ISO 9000 will affect their jobs. Make sure you stress what is in it for them. All must understand the meaning and requirements of ISO 9000 since everybody has to participate. The more people who understand ISO 9000 and know the benefits, the less resistance you'll face.

You can educate people through various departments (your ISO 9000 steering council members can spread the word), company-wide training courses, and through a regular company newsletter devoted to quality and ISO 9000.

Constant, consistent, and open communication with people is the key!

STEP 10: Develop ISO Quality Teams for Each Operational Area

This is a good way to get ISO 9000 information ingrained in your organization. These teams help discover and correct problems discovered at the lowest organizational levels.

STEP 11: Have a System to Upgrade Your Procedures

Your ISO 9000 steering council must develop and approve a system on how to upgrade procedures. The system must focus and be led by the employees who do the work. The employees must become part of the process. Any changes in procedures must be discussed and approved by all department employees. The procedures and records must be stored in a place that can be easily accessed.

The benefit of this step is that it promotes team spirit and employee involvement (strengthening commitment). It is also a good way to expose employees to new tasks.

TEP 12: Develop Corrective Action for Nonconformance

One ISO 9001 requirement (4.14) is the establishment of a corrective action process. You must have procedures in place to prevent recurrence of a problem.

You can do this through corrective action reports. Your internal auditor's goal is to identify the root cause of the discovered problem and ensure the department where the problem occurred that corrections will be made in an agreed-upon time frame.

This also has the added benefit of giving you and your employees the experience and confidence you need before your entire organization is audited by a third-party registrar.

STEP 13: Create and Train Internal Auditors

ISO 9001 (4.17) says you must periodically check your quality system with trained internal auditors. Mini-audit teams can check at the department level; a company-wide team can check at the company level. These auditors should follow the auditing guidelines set out in ISO 10001 (a part of the ISO 9000 series).

Not only will this satisfy an ISO 9000 series requirement, auditing is also a way to give you up-to-date feedback on how well or poorly your quality system is working. The auditor training and audit experience can create even more ISO 9000 experts in your organization.

Your audit teams should conduct periodic "mock audits" of departments and functional areas to check on your progress toward ISO 9000 readiness, and a company-wide team should conduct your first detailed internal audit prior to any audit visit from your registrar.

After you complete your first detailed internal audit, you should ask your registrar's lead auditor and audit team to conduct a mini-assessment of your facility. This will help you become familiar with the registar's audit approach and teach you and your auditors how to conduct formal compliance reviews yourself.

Most registars recommend such a preassessment; some will require it. It's a good learning experience, so do it.

Sometime before your final assessment, your company-wide audit team should re-audit the entire facility.

STEP 14: Final Assessment

This is it. You should be ready. You've checked all of your procedures, documents, and records for compliance to the particular ISO 9000 standard certification you've applied for.

This step occurs sometime after the registrar's preassessment or after the registrar determines that your documented quality system and manual conform to the ISO 9000 standard you have selected.

This final audit typically consists of two or three auditors (depending on the size of your organization) who'll spend two to four days at your facility.

The registrar's assessment will result in one of three actions:

- *Disapproval.* Disapproval comes either when your quality system is well documented but hasn't been implemented or when you haven't addressed basic elements such as internal auditing, corrective action, or process control. This will mean you'll have to go through the registrar's re-evaluation.

- *Conditional or Provisional Approval.* You'll get conditional or provisional approval if you've addressed all elements of the standard and have systems documented but not fully implemented; or if there are several deficiencies found in an area showing a "negative trend" (an area that needs further attention).

FOURTEEN STEPS TO CERTIFICATION (continued)

Conditional approval means you have to correct deficiencies within a registrar-defined time frame. After reviewing the subsequent corrective action, the registrar can either re-evaluate or accept the corrective action and review its implementation during future surveillance visits that will come about every six months. Should the registrar find serious nonconformance with ISO 9000 standards and registrar rules, your registration can be canceled.

- *Approval.* You'll get certified if you have implemented all elements associated with ISO 9001, 9002, or 9003 with only minor deficiencies noted during the assessment. If approved, you get a certificate of registration for the facility registered and ISO standard used. You can then use the certificate number and symbol on your advertising and correspondence. The registrar lists you in its directory identifying facility location, ISO standard used, and certificate number. Again, for continuing certification, you must expect registrar surveillance audits about every six months and a formal re-audit every three years.

DEVELOP YOUR CUSTOMIZED READINESS-ASSESSMENT CHECKLISTS

Do you think your organization is ready for the fine-toothed comb of your internal auditors? The registrar?

Each of the major operational areas within your business should use the following framework to develop a checklist to assess its readiness. You and your people will have to review carefully each of the 20 elements described earlier to come up with appropriate questions for your company for each element of either ISO 9001, ISO 9002, or ISO 9003; however, appropriate ISO elements for each major operational unit are suggested in the following section.

To get you started, sample questions appear for the first ISO item (4.1, Management responsibility) that your company's management might consider. Make sure you tailor the questions to your company and industry. If the departments are not in compliance with any of the items, they should indicate what they must do to become ready and when they will do it.

The finished checklists will serve as a good guide for your internal auditors and are designed for everybody to learn what ISO 9000 elements really ask for.

- ☐ Have you documented a clear quality policy and corporate mission?
- ☐ Have you assigned an ISO 9000 program manager?
- ☐ Are you training everybody to understand your quality policy and are you maintaining it properly?
- ☐ Have you created or revised job descriptions so they define quality authority and responsibility?
- ☐ Do you have trained auditors and are their reports given to senior management?
- ☐ Has management reviewed all final inspection and test procedures to make sure they comply with customer contracts?
- ☐ Do managers regularly review your total quality system?
- ☐ Do you have a senior management representative who can solve problems according to procedures?
- ☐ Do you have enough trained people for verification?
- ☐ How does your management assure compliance with ISO 9000 standards?

READINESS-ASSESSMENT CHECKLISTS (continued)

Using the preceding questions as samples, go on to create appropriate questions for the ISO elements important to each of your company's departments.

MANAGEMENT

4.1 Management responsibility
4.3 Contract review
4.4 Design control
4.5 Document control
4.13 Control of nonconforming product
4.16 Quality records
4.17 Internal quality audits
4.18 Training

ORDER PROCESSING

4.1 Management responsibility
4.3 Contract review
4.5 Document control
4.13 Control of nonconforming product
4.14 Corrective action
4.16 Quality records
4.17 Internal quality audits
4.18 Training

RESEARCH, DESIGN, AND DEVELOPMENT

4.1 Management responsibility
4.2 Quality system
4.3 Contract review
4.4 Design control
4.5 Document control
4.6 Purchasing
4.8 Product identification and traceability
4.10 Inspection and testing
4.11 Inspection, measuring, and test equipment
4.16 Quality records
4.18 Training
4.20 Statistical techniques

PLANNING

4.1 Management responsibility
4.2 Quality system
4.4 Design control
4.5 Document control
4.6 Purchasing
4.7 Purchaser-supplied product
4.9 Process control
4.10 Inspection and testing
4.11 Inspection, measuring, and test equipment
4.16 Quality records
4.18 Training
4.20 Statistical techniques

PROCUREMENT

4.1 Management responsibility
4.2 Quality system
4.4 Design control
4.5 Document control
4.6 Purchasing
4.16 Quality records
4.18 Training
4.20 Statistical techniques

STORES & MATERIAL HANDLING

4.1 Management responsibility
4.2 Quality system
4.5 Document control
4.6 Purchasing
4.9 Process control
4.12 Inspection and test status
4.13 Control of nonconforming product
4.14 Corrective action
4.15 Handling, storage, packaging, and delivery
4.16 Quality records
4.20 Statistical techniques

READINESS-ASSESSMENT CHECKLISTS (continued)

PRODUCTION

4.1 Management responsibility
4.2 Quality system
4.4 Design control
4.5 Document control
4.6 Purchasing
4.8 Product identification and traceability
4.9 Process control
4.10 Inspection and testing
4.11 Inspection, measuring and test equipment
4.12 Inspection and test status
4.13 Control of nonconforming product
4.14 Corrective action
4.15 Handling, storage, packaging, and delivery
4.16 Quality records
4.18 Training
4.20 Statistical techniques

INSPECTION

4.1 Management responsibility
4.3 Contract review
4.4 Design control
4.5 Document control
4.8 Product identification and traceability
4.9 Process control
4.10 Inspection and testing
4.11 Inspection, measuring, and test equipment
4.12 Inspection and test status
4.13 Control of nonconforming product
4.14 Corrective action
4.16 Quality records
4.18 Training
4.20 Statistical techniques

SHIPPING AND TRANSPORTATION

4.1 Management responsibility
4.3 Contract review
4.5 Document control
4.8 Product identification and traceability
4.12 Inspection and test status
4.15 Handling, storage, packaging, and delivery
4.16 Quality records
4.18 Training

SERVICING

4.1 Management responsibility
4.3 Contract review
4.5 Document control
4.8 Product identification and traceability
4.9 Process control
4.10 Inspection and testing
4.11 Inspection, measuring and test equipment
4.12 Inspection and test status
4.13 Control of nonconforming product
4.15 Handling, storage, packaging, and delivery
4.16 Quality records
4.18 Training
4.19 Servicing

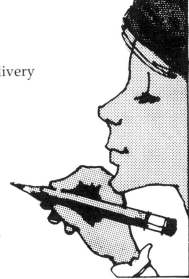

THE MOST FREQUENTLY ASKED QUESTIONS ABOUT ISO 9000

1. Our facility gets certified in an ISO 9000 standard. Shortly afterward, our advertising people start touting our product as having ISO-certified quality. Is there anything wrong with this?

Yes, there is! ISO 9000 series certification is for the quality process, *not the* product. *Advertising that your ISO 9000 certification is for your product will force your registrar to revoke your certification.*

2. Once our facility is certified to an ISO 9000 standard, do we need to worry about keeping our quality processes and procedures up to date?

Yes! Remember, your registrar will audit your facility for ISO 9000 compliance about every six months. You will need to be recertified, usually every three years.

3. To improve our chances to get certified, is it best to bombard our registrar with a lengthy quality manual?

No. More is not necessarily better. The essential test the registrar applies is, "Do they do what they say they do?"

4. Is it best to go through a few practice internal audits before our registrar visits for the final audit?

Yes. And if you ask, your registrar will normally conduct a pre-assessment audit of your facility. This is a good idea, since you will find out more about how your registrar thinks and what he or she is looking for.

5. Is it easy to sidetrack our registrar?

No. Taking them to lunch, offering bribes, and otherwise stalling auditors will not work. Auditors will work until done and then charge you for the overtime. It is a lot easier just to cooperate. If you think you need to stall the auditors, you should rethink your need and readiness for ISO 9000.

6. Should I and the other managers write the quality assurance manual, policies, procedures and work instructions?

No. You should get as much input as possible from the people who actually do the work on the line. Yet leadership must play a key role in getting the ISO 9000 started and maintained.

7. What should I do if I see an ISO 9000-certified company not following its internal quality policy?

The first thing you should do is diplomatically tell the leadership you saw a problem. If the problem persists and is serious, you may have to contact the registrar. This is especially critical if the company is one of your suppliers.

8. How similar is ISO 9000 to the Malcolm Baldrige National Quality Award?

ISO 9000 covers roughly the same area as the Baldrige Category 5—Quality Assurance. If eventually you want to go for the Malcolm Baldrige Award, go for the ISO 9000 first.

9. Is ISO 9000 a European trade barrier?

This is a tricky question. There is always a chance that the trade laws of the European Community could be changed at a moment's notice to require ISO 9000 certification for market entry. If you are doing business worldwide, and especially in Europe, it just makes good sense to get ISO 9000 certified. The best thing to do is keep current with your markets and customers.

10. Our best customer, a large company, is considering becoming ISO 9000 certified. What should we do?

If you want to keep its business, it is in your best interest to start planning your own ISO 9000 certification. Once companies get certified, they tend to want the certification from their suppliers.

THE MOST FREQUENTLY ASKED QUESTIONS ABOUT ISO 9000 (continued)

11. Can we pick a registrar out of the yellow pages?

No. A good place to turn to for a list of competent ISO 9000 consultants is the American Society for Quality Control in Milwaukee, Wisconsin.

12. What should we look for?

First find out if the registrar has experience in your industry. Second, find out if he or she is accredited by a body recognized in the countries where you will export. Third, ask for price quotes. Finally, interview the registrar as you would a job candidate. Make sure you are comfortable with this person, because you will be together for a while.

13. Can our registrar also act as our consultant?

No! The registrar must remain separate from the consulting process. But if you do your homework, any consultant you work with should be able to get you to the point of certification within 12 to 18 months.

CONCLUSION

You know that to get certified in one of the ISO 9000 standards takes hard work, time, money, and documentation. You can't get away with a "seat of the pants" approach; if ISO is worth anything, it is worth the structured discipline that comes with it.

If you have the commitment (and that's really what it takes), go for it. But remember, getting ISO 9000 certification is not an end. Continuous quality improvement goes on and on (and just to keep you honest, remember those registrar surveillance audits come about every six months).

S E C T I O N

V

ISO 9000
Reference
Handbook

"The true opportunity for improvement in a product is in design—not materials, not manufacture."

—Unknown

DETAILS OF THE ISO 9000 SERIES ELEMENTS

The following explanation (offset in italic type) of the 20 elements in ISO 9001 comes from a variety of sources such as Dean Hawley, president of Attexor of Tucson, Arizona; John T. Rabbitt and Peter A. Bergh in the *ISO 9000 Book*; and my own interpretations.

4.0 QUALITY SYSTEM REQUIREMENTS

4.1 MANAGEMENT RESPONSIBILITY

Juran, Deming, and other quality gurus believe 80% to 90% of all problems can be traced back to management. Most ISO 9000 audit failures can ultimately be traced back to a problem with management too.

4.1.1 Quality Policy

The supplier's management that has executive responsibility for quality shall define and document its policy for quality including objectives for quality and its commitment to quality. The quality policy shall be relevant to the supplier's organizational goals and the expectations and needs of its customers. The supplier shall ensure that this policy is understood, implemented, and maintained at all levels in the organization.

The quality policy is a statement of commitment to quality from the highest level of corporate management. The quality policy also defines objectives pertaining to product quality.

4.1.2 Organization

4.1.2.1 Responsibility and Authority

The responsibility, authority and the interrelation of all personnel who manage, perform, and verify work affecting quality shall be defined; particularly for personnel who need the organizational freedom and authority to:

(a) initiate action to prevent the occurrence of product nonconformities relating to product, process, and quality system;

(b) identify and record any product, process, and quality system problems;

(c) initiate, recommend, or provide solutions through designated channels;

(d) verify the implementation of solutions;

(e) control further processing, delivery, or installation of nonconforming product until the deficiency or unsatisfactory condition has been corrected.

An organizational chart is the most effective way to define the relationship of key personnel. Procedures dealing with specific actions should define the authority and responsibility of the personnel concerned with these actions.

4.1.2.2 *Resources*

The supplier shall identify resource requirements, provide adequate resources and assign trained personnel (see 4.18) for management, performance of work, and verification activities including internal quality audits.

Fortunately, suppliers have the freedom to define the extent and scope of their own verification needs and methods since the verification activities are usually the most costly part of any quality system. Suppliers should take into account the nature of their products, their experience with the design and manufacture of the products, required manufacturing equipment and processes, contract requirements, any regulatory requirements, and customer satisfaction history.

To verify compliance with this standard, a quality auditor will be searching for evidence of written criteria for selection of suitable test and inspection equipment and the qualifications of the personnel carrying out the verification activities.

4.1.2.3 *Management Representative*

The supplier's management that has executive responsibility for quality shall appoint a member of its own management who, irrespective of other responsibilities, shall have defined authority for:

(a) ensuring that quality system requirements are established, implemented, and maintained in accordance with this International Standard,
(b) reporting on the performance of the quality system to the supplier's management for review and as a basis for improvement of the quality system.

Note: The responsibility of a management representative may also include liaison with external bodies on matters relating to the supplier's quality system.

This representative is usually a QA vice president, director, or manager in companies that have a structured quality system. His or her main role is responsibility for the quality system's compliance with ISO 9000. Although small companies are not required to maintain a full-time quality assurance manager, the person responsible for the QA function must have sufficient authority to enforce the standard's requirements effectively and to ensure that the quality system is in no way compromised when in conflict with other design/manufacturing interests.

4.1.3 **Management Review**

The supplier's management that has executive responsibility for quality shall review the quality system at defined intervals sufficient to ensure its continuing suitability and effectiveness in satisfying the requirements of this International Standard and the supplier's stated quality policy and objectives (see 4.1.1). Records of such reviews shall be maintained (see 4.16).

DETAILS OF THE ISO 9000 SERIES ELEMENTS (continued)

These reviews should not be confused with the reviews of the internal audits performed by personnel responsible for coordinating and administering the quality system. Management reviews, being broader in scope, are concerned with issues such as performance of the quality system and the cost of the quality system maintenance versus the quality benefits. These issues are in addition to the analysis of the internal audit results.

> **Note:** Although yearly management reviews are recommended for mature quality systems, newly implemented systems may require more frequent assessments.

4.2 QUALITY SYSTEM

4.2.1 *General*

The supplier shall establish and maintain a quality system as a means of ensuring the product conforms to specified requirements. The outline structure of the documentation covering the quality system requirements of this International Standard shall be defined in a quality manual. The quality manual shall include or reference the documented procedures that form part of the quality system.

> **Note:** Guidance on quality manuals is given in ISO 10013.

4.2.2 *Quality System Procedures*

The supplier shall:

(a) prepare documented procedures consistent with the requirements of this International Standard and the supplier's stated quality policy;
(b) effectively implement the documented procedures and the quality system.

For the purpose of this International Standard the degree of documentation required for the procedures that form part of the quality system shall depend on the methods used, skills needed, and the training acquired by personnel involved in carrying out the activity.

Implementation is assessed against the system documentation. Therefore, compliance is achieved in a two-step approach. First, documentation comprising manuals, procedures, and instructions that define and regulate the quality system must be established. Second, the system must be implemented. In assessing quality systems, auditors will review the documentation against the standard, and then the implementation of the quality system against the documentation.

In sum, the quality system must be established, documented, and maintained. In addition, you must ensure that products meet customer requirements, include documented quality-system procedures and instructions, and see that the requirements of the International Standard are implemented effectively.

Note: The ISO International Standards are not industry specific. The knowledgeable supplier will design the quality system and technical standards to meet the expectations of the customers.

4.2.3 Quality Planning

The supplier shall define and document how the requirements for quality will be met. Quality planning shall be consistent with all other requirements of a supplier's quality system and shall be documented in a format to suit the supplier's method of operation. The supplier shall give timely consideration to the following activities, as appropriate, in meeting the specified requirements for products, projects, or contracts:

(a) the preparation of quality plans
(b) the identification and acquisition of any controls, processes, inspection equipment, fixtures, total production resources, and skills that may be needed to achieve the required quality

DETAILS OF THE ISO 9000 SERIES ELEMENTS (continued)

(c) ensuring the compatibility of the design, the production process, installation, servicing, inspection and test procedures, and the applicable documentation

(d) the updating as necessary of quality control, inspection and testing techniques, including the development of new instrumentation

(e) the identification of any measurement requirement involving capability that exceeds the known state of the art in sufficient time for the needed capability to be developed

(f) the identification of suitable verification at appropriate stages in the product realization

(g) the clarification of standards of acceptability for all features and requirements, including those which contain a subjective element

(h) the identification and preparation of quality records (see 4.16)

> **Note:** The quality plans referred to (see 4.2.3a) may be in the form of a reference to the appropriate documented procedures that form an integral part of the supplier's quality system.

4.3 CONTRACT REVIEW

4.3.1 General

The supplier shall establish and maintain procedures for contract review and for the coordination of these activities.

4.3.2 Review

Each accepted tender, contract, and order (statement of requirement) shall be reviewed by the supplier to ensure that:

(a) the requirements are adequately defined and documented. Where no written statement of requirement is available for a verbal order, the supplier shall ensure that the order requirements are agreed upon before their acceptance

(b) any contract or accepted order requirements differing from those in their tender are resolved

(c) the suppliers can meet contracted or accepted order requirements

4.3.3 Amendment to Contract

The supplier shall identify how amendment to a contract is made and correctly transferred to functions concerned within the supplier's organization.

4.3.4 Records

Records of such contract reviews shall be maintained (see 4.16).

Note 1: Channels for communication with the customer's organization in these contract matters should be established.

Note 2: For the purpose of this International Standard, the terms "contract" or "accepted order" are defined as "agreed requirements between a supplier and customer transmitted by any means."

Suppliers must assure themselves that they fully understand the purchaser's requirements. For standard products, the suppliers need to confirm that the purchase orders received are complete and contain no obvious errors. However, for custom (nonstandard) products, the designer/manufacturer will often have to help the purchaser in defining the specifications. When the requirements are stated in terms of a desired result instead of a technical specification, full understanding of what the purchaser actually wants may be a project in itself. Although these two scenarios are at opposite ends of the spectrum, the goals are the same—complete understanding of the purchaser's order.

4.4 DESIGN CONTROL

Note: ISO 9000's recognition of the strong relationship between product design and product quality is reflected in this standard. The major difference between ISO 9001 and ISO 9002 is the absence of Section 4.4 (Design control) from ISO 9002.

DETAILS OF THE ISO 9000 SERIES ELEMENTS (continued)

4.4.1 *General*

Suppliers shall establish and maintain documented procedures to control and verify the design of the product in order to ensure that the specified requirements are met.

Design control requires manufacturers to establish and carry out a formal process that takes product design through a series of steps, from formulation of product requirements and specifications, through product testing and process validation. Manufacturers are required to describe product development by means of comprehensive procedures, follow those procedures, and produce verifying documentation to demonstrate procedural compliance.

Design control systems can be tailored according to the product being developed. Procedures for simple products need not be as elaborate as those for complex products in which a design error could have catastrophic results. **However, the goal at every step in product development should be to identify and isolate potential weaknesses.**

Design control also pertains to products already in production. For products already being produced, the application of design control procedures to such products or processes ensures that changes are carefully reviewed, properly tested or validated, and receive the same high level of scrutiny as the product or process did at its beginning. Properly applied to products being manufactured, design control ensures that product safety, reliability, performance, labeling and, if applicable, packaging, are not compromised, and that any proposed changes produce the desired results.

Note: It is tempting to either overdocument procedures, which produces a poor understanding of design control procedures by company and auditing bodies alike, or to cut corners by deviating from prescribed practices. Instead, an effective approach to design control is to construct a relatively simple set of procedures and modify them based on experience.

4.4.2 *Design and Development Planning*

The supplier shall prepare plans for each design and development activity, including defined responsibility, and describe or reference these activities. The design and development activities shall be assigned to qualified personnel equipped with adequate resources. The plans shall be updated as the design evolves.

The first phase of designing a new product is design and development planning. This phase is critical because it establishes the groundwork for the design process.

4.4.3 *Organizational and Technical Interfaces*

Organizational and technical interfaces between different groups that have input to the design process shall be defined and the necessary information documented, transmitted, and regularly reviewed.

The object of design and development planning is to make sure that the design process is properly planned. Design and development planning makes clear what is going to happen, who is responsible for making it happen, and the timetable defining when it will happen.

The Project Proposal *The product development process begins when an idea for a new product is presented to management. If the product seems promising, management instructs representatives from such areas as marketing, engineering, and manufacturing to investigate whether it is feasible (benefits outweigh risks) to develop the product.*

After the research is completed, the various department representatives produce a project proposal—the document recommending whether or not to develop the product and the various conditions related to its manufacture. Management reviews the proposal and decides whether to go ahead with the project or cancel it.

DETAILS OF THE ISO 9000 SERIES ELEMENTS (continued)

Once management decides that a project is worth pursuing, product development planning can actually begin. Management assigns a project team to plan a program for the product's design, development, and manufacture. This team is comprised of a project manager, group managers who report to the project manager, and various departments who will be involved in the product design.

> **Note:** Selection of a good overall project manager is crucial to the success of planning the project. *The project manager holds the ultimate responsiblity for the course of the product's development.* Committee management does not work.
>
> "When everybody is responsible, nobody is responsible."
>
> —Anonymous

Regular meetings must be scheduled and minutes taken to track the status of project planning. Minutes must be published and distributed to notify team members of pending action items and provide project status information.

The Project Plan *The overall project plan identifies, in general terms, the network of activities, personnel, and resources that will be involved in the design and development process. The project plan organizes and documents the design process, breaking it down into manageable stages that deal with design: input, output, verification, and transfer.*

Flow diagrams such as PERT (program evaluation/review technique) and checklists help ensure that the project plan goals (cutting project costs, reducing time necessary for completion, improvement of scheduling of personnel and resources, ability to anticipate problems, develop better troubleshooting techniques, and so on) are met.

4.4.4 Design Input

Design input requirements relating to the product, including applicable statutory and regulatory requirements, shall be identified, documented, and their selection reviewed by the supplier for adequacy. Incomplete, ambiguous, or conflicting requirements shall be resolved with those responsible for imposing these requirements. Design input shall take into consideration the results of any contract review activities.

There can be no quality product if its designers do not fully understand the needs of its users and/or are not able to translate those needs into a set of desired product features and characteristics.

Briefly stated, design input is all the information that goes into the design of a product. At this project stage, the project manager needs to schedule extensive use of people from marketing, engineering, manufacturing, and quality control. The project manager must also schedule design reviews as required during—and between—each phase of design development.

Design input is the backbone of the product-development process. It is this phase in which the manufacturer gathers information about the performance requirements for the intended product and defines the preliminary specifications for the design characteristics, materials composition, and the operational configuration of the product. All requirements relating to the product must be identified, documented, and their selection reviewed by the manufacturer for adequacy.

The goal of the design-input phase is a report that establishes acceptable preliminary specifications for a product to be developed. This report is a "design description document" or "product brief." The specifications set forth in this report must be as comprehensive and precise as possible. It should address all factors necessary to describe the product:

- *design characteristics*
- *materials*
- *manufacturability*

- *testing and validation*
- *installation*
- *servicing*

DETAILS OF THE ISO 9000 SERIES ELEMENTS (continued)

This phase of the design-control process should involve all groups that are necessary to good decision making, resource allocation, and overall project management. Manufacturers should consider the following when developing the product proposal:

- *User performance expectations (operational speed, ease of use)*

- *Technological viability (manual/semiautomatic/automatic—what price is the customer willing to pay)*

- *Safety (safety features required to protect the user)*

- *Reliability (will the systems function as designed; what about product reliability over time or under harsh environmental conditions?)*

Sources of Information *Generally, market research tends to gather information only from outside sources—identifiable users, trade associations, etc. However, valuable resources usually exist within a company in the form of long-term employees who have previously participated in product development activities. A company's internal records can also be a reliable source of information for guiding the design and development process, especially when the product under consideration is an updated version of a product already being manufactured. Customer complaints, complaint evaluations, records of manufacturing problems, and so on, may all contribute to defining the specifications for a new product.*

Service records are another source of information frequently over-looked. When service problems are reported to the manufacturer, or when service technicians resolve reported problems, such information should be compiled so that it is available when the development research team begins the design-input phase.

Customer satisfaction or customer preference interviews can also help develop data concerning perceived customer needs and requirements.

Manufacturability *Often, development teams fail to consider whether the product under development is actually manufacturable under current manufacturing capabilities and resources, leaving this question to be answered when the product is ready to be released to the manufacturing group. It is imperative that the product-development group determine very early in the design and development stage whether the company will need to modify its facilities, purchase new equipment, or hire additional manufacturing personnel. These factors are costly and can cause delays in the production schedule if long lead times are required for the receipt of new equipment or facility renovation.*

Formalizing the Report *Once the research phase has been completed, all resulting data should be organized, analyzed, and a report prepared. This report establishes the preliminary specifications for the product and should include criteria for all aspects of the product previously identified. The general outline of the report should incorporate the following factors:*

- *Product identification (including the company name)*

- *User safety requirements*

- *Identifiable performance factors and expectations*

- *Physical characteristics*

- *Requirements for compatibility with other products in the product line*

- *Environmental requirements/limitations*

- *Labeling requirements (control panels, hazard warnings)*

4.4.5 Design Review

At appropriate stages of design, formal documented reviews of the design results shall be planned and conducted. Participants at each design review shall include representatives of all functions concerned with the design stage being reviewed as well as other specialist personnel, as required. Records of such reviews shall be maintained (see 4.16).

DETAILS OF THE ISO 9000 SERIES ELEMENTS (continued)

4.4.6 Design Output

Design output shall be documented and expressed in terms of requirements that can be verified.

Design output shall:

(a) meet the design-input requirements
(b) contain or reference acceptance criteria
(c) identify those characteristics of the design that are crucial to the safe and proper functioning of the product (such as operating, storage, handling, maintenance, and disposal requirements)
(d) include a review of design output documents before release

Design output is the creation of product and process documentation and the transformation of product descriptions/specifications into one or more fully developed prototypes/models that can be tested against specifications. Design output defines the product, instructs how to manufacture it (purchasing, production, installation, testing, inspection, and servicing) and provides evidence of compliance with input requirements.

Design output is usually expressed in terms of drawings, specifications, work instructions, and procedures. However, test plans and reports should also be used to verify that a product meets the design-input requirements. Another requirement is determining the acceptance criteria—tolerances, surface finish, workmanship, and acceptability criteria for inspection and test results.

Crucial design characteristics must also be defined and documented. Identification of crucial characteristics is evidence that the designers have analyzed the design and desire to communicate to manufacturing what is important and where the most intensive quality effort should be concentrated. To demonstrate compliance with this requirement, certain dimensions, welds, and so on can be highlighted or labeled "critical" in specifications or drawings.

The design-output stage also includes the plans for creating technical and user manuals, and materials and vendor selection.

For planning purposes, it is helpful to divide documentation into categories. This helps the design team determine what documents are required, why they are needed, who will produce them, and when in the development cycle they should be produced. Useful design output documentation categories are performance and safety characteristics in addition to product and process documentation.

Performance Characteristics   Early in the development process, the design team should begin writing plans for validating product performance. This should include test plans for performance, environment, and reliability.

Performance Test Plan   The object of the performance test plan is to validate the product features as defined in the design input. Test plans generally define what characteristics will be tested, as opposed to how the tests will be conducted. Where possible, product features should be verified at the extreme limits of their specifications.

Environmental Test Plan   The object of the environmental test plan is to define the product's operating environment and customer requirements. These conditions can include temperature and/or humidity range and, in the case of military, storage environment. The test plan should take into consideration the "worst case" operating or test conditions.

Reliability Test Plan   The reliability test plan should describe what methods will be used to determine mean time between failures and any other measures of reliability.

Safety Characteristics   Documents regarding safety characteristics typically include hazards analysis and the safety test plan.

DETAILS OF THE ISO 9000 SERIES ELEMENTS (continued)

Hazards Analysis   A hazards analysis should be conducted early in the design process. To produce safe products, the designers must know potential hazards, such as electrical, noise, air pressure, or breathing air. Developing a hazards analysis consists of the following:

- *Identifying a potential hazard*

- *Determining the potential cause*

- *Describing the minimum acceptable performance requirements*

- *Determining the method of control (design or labeling)*

- *Identifying potential solutions*

Safety Test Plan   The safety test plan outlines the protocol used to verify that a product or system conforms to safety standards. It includes content requirements for labels and documentation, protection against electrical, mechanical, and other types of hazards.

Product Documentation   *Product documentation defines the product structure. Its content is highly influenced by the type and complexity of the product, and includes such items as:*

- *top-level assembly drawings*
- *component drawings and specifications*
- *bill of materials*
- *labeling*

Top-Level Assembly Drawings   Top-level assembly drawings define the overall product structure. These documents enable the user to identify and organize all lower-level documents required to define a product completely. There is no standard format for top-level drawings; some combine a pictorial drawing and a bill of materials while others may consist of charts with only the drawing numbers identified.

Component Drawings and Specifications   Component drawings typically include drawings of fabricated components, etched circuit board drawings, schematic diagrams, packaging, artwork, and drawings of labels.

Component specifications refer to the documents used to describe common or off-the-shelf components. These documents can be data sheets or drawings generated by the manufacturers (suppliers) of a component.

Bill of Materials   A bill of materials is a list of components, assemblies, and other items required to define a product.

Labeling   Labeling includes the terminology that appears on the product, in product displays, the operator's manual, service and parts manual, data sheets, training materials/manuals, videotapes, advertising, and any other items that make claims about the product.

Process Documentation   Process documentation defines how a product will be produced. Its content is strongly influenced by the manufacturing process and by the company organization. Process documentation covers a broad range of activities, beginning with the receipt of materials and ending with the shipment of products.

This category of documentation is required to help the manufacturing area carry out its function. The type (and complexity) of process documentation depends upon the product and the level of automation and skill of the people involved in the process. The following items should be included in the design output: process-flow diagram, manufacturing instructions and procedures, and documentation defining manufacturing equipment.

Process-Flow Diagram   The process-flow diagram is a top-level drawing that defines the manufacturing process for a product. It shows the sequence of operations necessary to produce the product and is a useful tool for planning, describing, and documenting the manufacturing process. Process-flow diagrams show the series of operations used to define the tasks of each operating sequence in the manufacturing process.

DETAILS OF THE ISO 9000 SERIES ELEMENTS (continued)

Manufacturing Instructions and Procedures   Manufacturing procedures provide employees with detailed assembly, testing, inspection, and installation instructions. These procedures should be written for the lowest necessary skill level and should include any special tools or manufacturing materials needed to complete an operating sequence.

Documentation Defining Manufacturing Equipment   This category refers to the tools, machines, and fixtures necessary to perform manufacturing tasks or operations, including calibration and inspection. The manufacturing or engineering department generally selects or designs the needed manufacturing equipment during the process design phase of a project.

Documentation for the equipment must include specifications, calibration and maintenance requirements. It should also include the criteria for selecting the equipment, including the validation procedure and a report summarizing the results of the validation.

These documents are generated throughout the entire design phase. Documentation related to the safety and performance characteristics of a product is generated early in the design phase and is used by the engineering department to ensure that the safety requirements and performance characteristics listed in the product specifications are incorporated in the product design and validated prior to product release to manufacturing.

Note: A requirement of design output is that it must correspond to design input requirements. This requirement implies that there should be a mechanism for comparing the design input to the design output to ensure that all requirements have been accounted for and validated before a product is released to manufacturing.

4.4.7 *Design Verification*

At appropriate stages of design, design verification shall be performed to ensure that the design stage output meets the design stage input requirements. The design verification measures shall be recorded (see 4.16).

Note: In addition to conducting design reviews, design verification may include activities such as the following:

(a) performing alternative calculations
(b) comparing the new design with a similar proven design, if available
(c) undertaking tests and demonstrations
(d) reviewing the design stage documents before release

At this point, the product is usually ready to enter pilot production. This stage requires considerable involvement from engineering and manufacturing personnel to answer design questions, train operators, and resolve technical problems. Materials and quality assurance personnel also need to be involved to ensure that the materials meet specifications and that the manufacturing process is properly validated.

At the completion of the design verification, all documentation developed in the design process must be transferred to the manufacturing group that will build the product. This group includes personnel in materials, manufacturing, quality assurance, and engineering.

At the conclusion of the design transfer stage, project management needs to ensure that the product master record is in place and that all test plans and reports have been finalized and archived—in brief, everything verifying that design output meets design input.

DETAILS OF THE ISO 9000 SERIES ELEMENTS (continued)

4.4.8 Design Validation

Design validation shall be performed to ensure the product conforms to defined user needs and/or requirements.

Note 1: Design validation follows successful design verification (see 4.4.7).

Note 2: Validation is normally performed on the final product under defined operating conditions. It may be necessary in earlier stages. Multiple validations may be performed if there are different intended uses.

4.4.9 Design Changes

All design changes and modifications shall be identified, documented, reviewed, and approved by authorized personnel before their realization.

Appropriate channels for the initiation and approval of design changes and modifications must be established and described in relevant procedures. The importance of this requirement is the timely identification and correction of a problem stemming from a functional, safety, performance, or maintenance problem. Design changes may also come about from changes in customer needs, new product technology, or a need to increase product/component reliability.

Once the input requirements for a design change have been identified and documented, the design change activities should follow a process similar to the one described for the initial design. These activities should be planned, documented, and verified at appropriate stages. The document control system for design changes must permit revisions and reissues of technical documents, distribution of new documents, and the removal of obsolete documents.

4.5 DOCUMENT CONTROL

4.5.1 *General*

The supplier shall establish and maintain procedures to control all documents and data that relate to the requirements of this International Standard, including, to the extent applicable, documents of external origin such as standards and customer drawings.

Note: Documents and data can be in the form of hard copy media or they can be in electronic or other media.

Manufacturers must have in place a procedure for the clear and precise control of all documents required by the ISO standards. Such documents must be reviewed and approved by authorized personnel before they are issued for official use. They must also be available at the location where they are to be used, and procedures must be in place to remove obsolete documents promptly from their point of use.

Companies need to be able to distinguish between engineering drawings that are still being validated and those that have been released to production. Companies usually accomplish this by assigning numeric revision levels to documents that are in the development phase and alphabetic revision levels to documents issued for production.

It is also normal procedure to release individual drawings or groups of drawings to manufacturing throughout the design process. The official release date and distribution can be established as part of the engineering change order, with the signatures of the people authorized to release the document.

4.5.2 *Document Approval and Issue*

The documents and data shall be reviewed and approved for adequacy by authorized personnel prior to issue. A master list or equivalent document-control procedure identifying the current revision status of documents shall be established and be readily available to preclude the use of invalid and/or obsolete documents.

DETAILS OF THE ISO 9000 SERIES ELEMENTS (continued)

Controls shall also ensure that:

(a) the pertinent issues of appropriate documents are available wherever operations essential to the effective functioning of the quality system are performed
(b) invalid and/or obsolete documents are promptly removed from all points of issue or use, or otherwise assured against unintended use
(c) any obsolete documents retained for legal and/or knowledge preservation purposes are suitably identified

4.5.3 *Document Changes*

Changes to documents shall be reviewed and approved by the same functions/organizations that performed the original review and approval unless specifically designated otherwise. The designated functions/organizations shall have access to pertinent background information upon which to base their review and approval. Where practicable, the nature of the change shall be identified in the document or the appropriate attachments.

People involved in the engineering change order process are usually knowledgeable about company operations and can make sure that purchase orders and other activities associated with the release of a document are issued at the appropriate time. The change order process also marks the beginning of an audit trail for the document.

Hundreds of documents are produced during the development process. Some are historical and will be archived for future reference. Others, like product and process drawings, are referred to as "living documents" and will be updated throughout the life cycle of a product.

The development team should carefully consider the organization of documents created during the development cycle, including their type, content, purpose, and interrelatonship. Each document should be assigned a unique identification number. A sample identification number follows:

XXX-XXXX-XX

The first set (3 characters) identifies the category of a document. The second set (4 characters) is assigned sequentially within a category, and the last set (2 characters) reflects major revisions.

> **Note:** This standard also states that manufacturers should maintain a master list of documents that identifies their current revision level and also indicates nonapplicable or obsolete documents. One technique for organizing records is to develop a master record index for each product—a comprehensive list of design output documents, which should include a document or part number, description, revision level, location, and other important information.

This regulation has provisions for the approval, issuing, organization, archiving, accessibility and obsolescence of documents. Companies will probably also need to control formally design-related documentation such as engineering notebooks, design review notes, calculations, etc.

4.6   PURCHASING

4.6.1   *General*

The supplier shall establish and maintain documented procedures to ensure the purchased product (see 3.1) conforms to specified requirements.

DETAILS OF THE ISO 9000 SERIES ELEMENTS (continued)

4.6.2 *Evaluation of Subcontractors*

The supplier shall:

(a) evaluate and select subcontractors on the basis of their ability to meet subcontract requirements including quality system and quality assurance requirements
(b) define the type and extent of control exercised by the supplier over subcontractors. This shall depend upon the type of product, the impact of subcontracted product on the quality of final product and, where applicable, on the quality audit reports and/or quality records of subcontractors' previously demonstrated capability and performance
(c) establish and maintain quality records of acceptable subcontractors (see 4.16)

Subcontractors must be qualified to supply the ordered, described products. Essentially, subcontractors are an extension of the supplier, and therefore have in place quality-management systems equivalent to those of the supplier.

Subcontractors are assessed on their ability to meet the quality requirements of the product and on their performance history. The purchasing department must maintain an approved subcontractor list including objective evaluations of the subcontractors.

Note: Although subcontractors are not explicitly required to operate under an ISO 9000 system to qualify as an approved subcontractor, they should be encouraged to implement ISO 9000 systems. The supplier is responsible for the effectiveness of the subcontractor's quality controls.

4.6.3 *Purchasing Data*

Purchasing documents shall contain data clearly describing the product order, including, where applicable:

(a) the type, class, grade or other precise identification

(b) the title or other positive identification and applicable issue of specifications, drawings, process requirements, inspection instructions, and other relevant technical data, including requirements for approval or qualification of product, procedures, process equipment, and personnel

(c) the title, number, and issue of the quality system standard to be applied. The supplier shall review and approve purchasing documents for adequacy of specified requirements prior to release

When ordering products from subcontractors, the products must be clearly and completely described, and all quality verification-related requirements are to be on the purchase order.

Clarity and completeness of pertinent data are of extreme importance. Items to be purchased should be described as completely as possible using precise identifications. Specifications and drawings should be identified by title and date of issue.

If a qualification or audit of the subcontractor's processes, equipment, or personnel is required, it must be so stated on the purchase order.

Purchasing documents must be reviewed and approved prior to release to a subcontractor. Since the purpose of this verification is to ensure the adequacy of specific product requirements, the person who originated the request is usually the best suited to perform the verification.

4.6.4 *Verification of Purchased Product*

4.6.4.1 Supplier verification of subcontractors

> Where the supplier verifies the purchased product at the subcontractor's premises, the supplier shall specify verification arrangements and the method of product release in the purchasing documents.

DETAILS OF THE ISO 9000 SERIES
ELEMENTS (continued)

4.6.4.2 *Customer verification of subcontracted product*

Where specified in the contract, the supplier's customer or representative shall be afforded the right to verify at sub-contractor premises and the supplier's premises that subcontracted product conforms to specified requirements. Such verification shall not be used by the supplier as evidence of effective control of quality by the subcontractor.

Verification by the customer shall not absolve the supplier of the responsibility for providing an acceptable product nor shall it preclude subsequent rejection by the customer.

Verification by the customer does not absolve suppliers from responsibility. Suppliers maintain responsibility for product quality whether the inspection was made prior to shipment or upon receipt at the customer's premises. Supplier must state in their quality manuals that they retain the responsibility for product quality regardless of the customer's verifications.

4.7 PURCHASER-SUPPLIED PRODUCT

The supplier shall establish and maintain documented procedures for verification, storage, and maintenance of customer-supplied products provided for incorporation into the supplies. Any such product that is lost, damaged, or is otherwise unsuitable for use shall be recorded and reported to the customer (see 4.16).

Note: Verification by the supplier does not absolve the customer of the responsibility for providing an acceptable product.

Customer-supplied products may be tooling, fixtures, and so on, or even semifinished components, which have been supplied by the customer to the supplier for use by the supplier in manufacturing/assembling components for the customer.

Documenting compliance with this standard may be distributed throughout procedures dealing with other activities—handling of the customer-supplied product does not need a separate procedure.

> **Note:** The top-level QA manual should contain a section corresponding to Section 4.7 to avoid sectional numbering discrepancies between the QA manual and the standard.

4.8 PRODUCT IDENTIFICATION AND TRACEABILITY

Where appropriate, the supplier shall establish and maintain documented procedures for identifying the product by suitable means from receipt and during all stages of production, delivery, and installation.

Where and to the extent that traceability is a specified requirement, the supplier shall establish and maintain documented procedures for unique identification of individual products or batches. This identification shall be recorded (see 4.16).

The identification required by this standard should be traceable to specific drawings and/or technical specifications. Its purpose is to ensure that only specified components are used to assemble the product and that the identification system distinguishes between different grades of otherwise similar materials, components, or products. Do not confuse it with general product labeling, which is usually performed for commercial, accounting, or inventory reasons.

Traceability is a requirement only when specified by the purchaser or a third party, such as a government entity. On the documentation and implementation levels, traceability is usually handled as an extension of the basic identification system required by the first statement of this standard. Normally, there is no need for a separate set of procedures to document the identification and traceability systems respectively, unless it is necessary for other reasons.

DETAILS OF THE ISO 9000 SERIES ELEMENTS (continued)

4.9 PROCESS CONTROL

The supplier shall identify and plan the production, installation, and servicing processes which directly affect quality and shall ensure that these processes are carried out under controlled conditions. Controlled conditions shall include the following:

(a) documented procedures defining the manner of production, installation, and servicing, where the absence of such procedures could adversely affect quality
(b) use of suitable production, installation, and servicing equipment, suitable working environment
(c) compliance with reference standards/codes, quality plans, and/or documented procedures
(d) monitoring and control of suitable process parameters and product characteristics during production, installation, and servicing
(e) the approval of processes and equipment, as appropriate
(f) criteria for workmanship which shall be stipulated in the clearest practicable manner—e.g. written standards, representative samples, or illustrations
(g) suitable maintenance of equipment to ensure continuing process capability

Processes, the results of which cannot be fully verified by subsequent inspection and testing of the product and where, for example, processing deficiencies may become apparent only after the product is in use, shall be carried out by qualified operators and/or require continuous monitoring and control of process parameters to ensure that the specified requirements are met.

Note: Such processes requiring prequalification of their process capability are frequently referred to as special processes.

The requirements for any qualification of process operations including associated equipment and personnel (see 4.18) shall be specified.

Records shall be maintained for qualified processes, equipment, and personnel, as appropriate (see 4.16).

The term "process," as used in manufacturing, denotes all activities connected with production. In a service-type industry, it includes all steps necessary to perform a service.

Production planning is the key requirement of this standard. It relates to incoming materials and components, manufacturing processes, product logistics, inspection, etc. All aspects must be defined and communicated to production personnel.

Work instructions and process procedures may be issued and maintained by quality assurance, or directly by production. Although both ways are acceptable, leaving them to production may be the more practical method. Regardless of where the responsibility lies, they must still be established and controlled in compliance with Section 4.5 of the standard.

4.10 INSPECTION AND TESTING

4.10.1 General

The supplier shall establish and maintain documented procedures for inspection and testing activities in order to verify that the specified requirements for the product are met. The required inspecting and testing, and the records to be established, shall be documented in the quality plan or documented procedures.

4.10.2 Receiving Inspection and Testing

4.10.2.1 The supplier shall ensure that incoming product is not used or processed (except in the circumstances described in 4.10.2.3) until it has been inspected or otherwise verified as conforming to specified requirements. Verification shall be in accordance with the quality plan and/or documented procedure.

DETAILS OF THE ISO 9000 SERIES ELEMENTS (continued)

In this subsection, the supplier is not given a choice as to which incoming material/components may or may not require verification. All materials and components to be incorporated in the final product must be both separated (from approved stock) and verified. Although suppliers define their own verification needs, these decisions must be made in advance and documented in procedures or quality plans.

> **Note:** If the quality system and the final inspection program of the vendor is certified to comply with ISO 9000 or comparable standard, and the products are accompanied by certificates of conformance or inspection records, verification of incoming product can be met by a review of such certificates and records.

4.10.2.2   In determining the amount and nature of receiving inspection, consideration shall be given to the amount of control exercised at the subcontractor's premises and the recorded evidence of conformance provided.

4.10.2.3   Where incoming product is released for urgent production purposes prior to verification, it shall be positively identified and recorded (see 4.16) in order to permit immediate recall and replacement in the event of nonconformance to specified requirements.

4.10.3 In-Process Inspection and Testing

The supplier shall:

(a) inspect the test product as required by the quality plan and/or documented procedures
(b) hold the product until the required inspection and tests have been completed or necessary reports have been received and verified except when the product is released under positive recall procedures (see 4.10.2.3). Release under positive recall procedures shall not preclude the activities outlined in 4.10.3a

4.10.4 Final Inspection and Testing

The supplier shall carry out all final inspection and testing in accordance with the quality plan and/or documented procedures to complete the evidence of conformance of the finished product to the specified requirements.

The quality plan and/or documented procedures for final inspection and testing shall require that all specified inspection and tests, including those specified either on receipt of product or in process, have been carried out and that the results meet specified requirements.

No product shall be dispatched until all the activities specified in the quality plan and/or documented procedures have been satisfactorily completed and the associated data and documentation is available and authorized.

In summary, the two requirements of this standard are as follows: (1) final inspection must verify all previous inspections have been satisfactorily completed, and (2) finished products awaiting final inspection must be prevented from being transferred/shipped.

4.10.5 Final Inspection and Test Records

The supplier shall carry out all final inspection and testing in accordance with the quality plan and/or documented procedures to complete the evidence of conformance of the finished product to the specified requirements.

The quality plan and/or documented procedures for final inspection and testing shall require that all specified inspection and tests, including those specified either on receipt of product or in process, have been carried out and that the results meet specified requirements.

No product shall be dispatched until all the activities specified in the quality plan and/or documented procedures have been satisfactorily completed and the associated data and documentation are available and authorized.

DETAILS OF THE ISO 9000 SERIES ELEMENTS (continued)

This standard requires that each inspection (receiving, in process, or final) be recorded and the record preserved for a specified period of time in accordance with appropriate procedures. Also refer to Section 4.16.

4.11 INSPECTION, MEASURING, AND TEST EQUIPMENT

4.11.1 General

The supplier shall establish and maintain documented procedures to control, calibrate, and maintain inspection, measuring, and test equipment (including test software) used by the supplier to demonstrate the conformance of the product to the specified requirements. Inspection, measuring, and test equipment shall be used in a manner that ensures that measurement uncertainty is known and is consistent with the required measurement capability.

Where test software or comparative references such as test hardware is used as suitable forms of inspection they shall be checked, to prove that they are capable of verifying the acceptability of product, prior to release for use during production, installation, or servicing and shall be rechecked at prescribed intervals. The supplier shall establish the extent and frequency of such checks and shall maintain records as evidence of control (see 4.16). Where and to the extent that the availability of technical data pertaining to the measurement devices is a specified requirement, such data shall be made available, when required by the customer or customer's representative, for verification that the devices are functionally adequate.

4.11.2 Control Procedure

The supplier shall:

(a) determine the measurements to be made, the accuracy required, and select the appropriate inspection, measuring, and test equipment that is capable of the accuracy and precision necessary

(b) identify all inspection, measuring, and test equipment, including measuring devices that can affect product quality and calibrate and adjust them at prescribed intervals, or prior to use, against certified equipment having a known valid relationship to internationally or nationally recognized standards. Where no such standards exist, the basis used for calibration shall be documented

(c) define the process employed for the calibration of inspection, measuring, and test equipment including details of equipment type, unique identification, location, frequency of checks, check method, acceptance criteria, and the action to be taken when results are unsatisfactory

(d) identify inspection, measuring, and test equipment with a suitable indicator or approved identification record to show the calibration status

(e) maintain calibration records for inspection, measuring, and test equipment (see 4.16)

(f) assess and document the validity of previous inspection and test results when inspection, measuring, and test equipment is found to be out of calibration

(g) ensure that the environmental conditions are suitable for the calibration, inspections, measurements, and tests being carried out

(h) ensure that the handling, preservation, and storage of inspection, measuring, and test equipment is such that the accuracy and fitness for use is maintained

(i) safeguard inspection, measuring, and test facilities, including both test hardware and test software, from adjustments which invalidate the calibration setting

Note: The quality assurance requirements for measuring equipment given in ISO 10012 may be used for guidance.

Measuring equipment used only as a production aid, and where accuracy is irrelevant, may be exempted from the control and calibration system. Such equipment may include such items as electrical test probes and meters, supply line pressure gauges, etc. When such equipment is excluded from the calibration system, it should be clearly marked that it is not calibrated.

DETAILS OF THE ISO 9000 SERIES ELEMENTS (continued)

Regarding implementation of the calibration system, a computerized log listing all measuring equipment, identification, current status, location, calibration frequency, last and due calibration dates, specified and measured accuracy, and so on, is most helpful in maintaining compliance.

4.12 INSPECTION AND TEST STATUS

The inspection and test status of the product shall be identified by suitable means, which indicates the conformance or nonconformance of the product with regard to inspection and tests performed. The identification of inspection and test status shall be maintained, as defined in the quality plan and/or documented procedures, throughout production, installation, and servicing of the product to ensure that only a product that has passed the required inspections and tests or released under an authorized concession (see 4.13.2) is dispatched, used or installed.

The purpose of inspection-status identification labels is to inform the next operator in the manufacturing sequence that the last required inspection was performed and the product passed. Any identification system that achieves this goal is acceptable. Also, status identification that is signed and dated can serve as an inspection record, which may be filed with other documents required by the quality system.

4.13 CONTROL OF NONCONFORMING PRODUCT

4.13.1 General

The supplier shall establish and maintain procedures to ensure that the product that does not conform to specified requirements is prevented from unintended use or installation. Control shall provide for identification, documentation, evaluation, segregation (when practical), disposition of nonconforming products, and for notification to the functions concerned.

Although the identification and documentation of a nonconforming product would normally be the responsibility of the quality inspectors, it is practical and desirable that other personnel be encouraged to report nonconforming product conditions. However, appropriate procedures should regulate such reporting.

4.13.2 Nonconforming Product Review and Disposition

The responsibility for review and authority for the disposition of a nonconforming product shall be defined.

Nonconforming product shall be reviewed in accordance with documented procedures. The options are that it may be:

(a) reworked to meet the specified requirements
(b) accepted with or without repair by concession
(c) regraded for alternative applications
(d) rejected or scrapped

Where required by the contract, the proposed use or repair of a product (see 4.13.2b) that does not conform to specified requirements shall be reported for concession to the customer or customer's representative. The description of nonconformity that has been accepted, and of repairs, shall be recorded to denote the actual condition (see 4.16).

Repaired and/or reworked product shall be reinspected in accordance with the quality plan and/or documented procedure requirements.

The nonconformity review system must be flexible enough to deal with simple defects as well as major safety hazards. The procedures must further specify what actions shall be taken to close out the nonconformity reports and define authority for the disposition of the products. When drafting these procedures, it may be useful to divide the possible nonconformity problems into different classes or levels of authority for disposition.

4.14 CORRECTIVE ACTION

4.14.1 General

The supplier shall establish and maintain documented procedures for implementing corrective and preventive action.

DETAILS OF THE ISO 9000 SERIES ELEMENTS (continued)

Any corrective or preventive action taken to eliminate the causes of actual or potential nonconformities shall be to a degree appropriate to the magnitude of problems and commensurate to the risks encountered.

The supplier shall implement and record any changes in the documented procedures resulting from corrective and preventive action.

4.14.2 Corrective Action

The procedures for corrective action shall include:

(a) the effective handling of customer complaints and reports of product noncomformities
(b) investigating the cause of nonconformities relating to product, process, and quality system and recording the results of the investigation (see 4.16)
(c) determining the corrective action needed to eliminate the cause of nonconformities
(d) applying controls to ensure that corrective action is taken and that it is effective

4.14.3 Preventive Action

The procedures for preventive action shall include:

(a) the use of appropriate sources of information such as processes and work operations that affect product quality, concessions, audit results, quality records, service reports, and customer complaints to detect, analyze, and eliminate potential causes of nonconformities
(b) determining the steps needed to deal with any problems requiring preventive action
(c) initiating preventive action and applying controls to ensure that it is effective
(d) ensuring that relevant information on actions taken including changes to procedures is submitted for management review (see 4.1.3)

> **Note:** Whenever corrective actions change the operation of the quality system, affected manuals, procedures, instructions, and other quality documents must be revised accordingly.

4.15 HANDLING, STORAGE, PACKAGING, AND DELIVERY

4.15.1 General

The supplier shall establish and maintain documented procedures for handling, storage, packaging, preservation, and delivery of the product.

This section deals with the product after its final inspection. Procedures required by this section can be established on two levels: the first being the general commitment to compliance as stated in the QA manual; the second being the specific rules, instructions, and specifications issued in various formats directly by the production, storage, and shipping departments.

4.15.2 Handling

The supplier shall provide methods of handling product that prevent damage or deterioration.

Handling methods include both the lifting/handling mechanisms (scheduled maintenance, inspection) and the training of personnel (instruction, testing, certification) to enhance both product and personnel safety. Each department responsible for the various handling processes should be encouraged to write and maintain its own procedures.

4.15.3 Storage

The supplier shall use designated storage areas or stock rooms to prevent damage or deterioration of product, pending use or delivery. Appropriate methods for authorizing receipt and the dispatch to and from such areas shall be stipulated.

In order to detect deterioration, the condition of product in stock shall be assessed at appropriate intervals.

DETAILS OF THE ISO 9000 SERIES ELEMENTS (continued)

The three basic requirements of this section are as follows: (1) storage areas are adequate and secure, (2) the movement of goods in and out of the storage areas is controlled, and (3) the condition of the goods is assessed regularly. A serious but common noncompliance with this standard is the mixing of materials, components, finished goods, and even scrap throughout the facility. When practical, storage areas should be physically separated and secured.

Size or other characteristics may prevent some products from being stored in the designated storage area; however, this does not exempt them from the requirements for adequate protection and movement control.

4.15.4 *Packaging*

The supplier shall control packing, packaging, and marking processes (including material used) to the extent necessary to ensure conformance to specified requirements.

Requirements for packaging control are similar to those applicable to other production processes. Packaging specifications should be documented, appropriate materials and equipment available, and personnel qualified. Any deviations from approved packaging must be authorized. Packaging procedures may be formalized on two levels: one defining the general requirements, authority, and responsibility; the other specifications and work instructions established and maintained by the packing or shipping department.

4.15.5 *Preservation*

Appropriate methods for preservation and segregation of product shall be applied when such product is under the supplier's control.

4.15.6 *Delivery*

The supplier shall arrange for the protection of the quality of product after final inspection and test. Where contractually specified, this protection shall be extended to include delivery to destination.

When delivery is a specified requirement of the contract, the department responsible for delivery will be audited against the entire standard. Whether or not delivery is a specified part of the contract, the supplier still has the responsibility to provide packaging suitable for the intended means of delivery.

4.16 QUALITY RECORDS

The supplier shall establish and maintain documented procedures for identification, collection, indexing, access, filing, storage, maintenance, and disposition of quality records.

Quality records shall be maintained to demonstrate conformance to specified requirements and the effective operation of the quality system. Pertinent subcontractor quality records shall be an element of these data.

All quality records shall be legible and shall be stored and retained in such a way that they are readily retrievable in facilities that provide a suitable environment to minimize deterioration or damage and to prevent loss.

Retention times of quality records shall be established and recorded. Where agreed contractually, quality records shall be made available for evaluation by the customer or a representative for an agreed-upon period.

Note: Records can be in the form of hard copy media, or they can be in electronic or other media.

Validation records provide documented evidence that a company's manufacturing processes consistently produce products that meet predetermined specifications and quality standards. Records also provide data for tracking trends and demonstrating performance of the quality system.

DETAILS OF THE ISO 9000 SERIES ELEMENTS (continued)

Four principal requirements comprise this section: (1) the record must be identifiable and legible; (2) the record must be easily retrievable; (3) the record should be stored appropriately and securely; and (4) the record must be retained for a specified period of time. Most noncompliance problems with this section involve the retrievability of a record. This is due in part to the fact that in many organizations specific product-related records are retained in various departments—purchasing, engineering, production control, quality control—leading to a chaotic (and usually unsuccessful) search to satisfy an auditor's simple request to produce a specific product's history record.

The validation report should effectively communicate the results of the validation study, explaining its objective, results, and how those results affirm or deny the acceptance criteria.

> **Note:** Data from a carefully recorded study report can be used to support changes in the product or processes.

A validation report should include the following: background, objective, summary, and conclusions and recommendations.

Background   *In this section, briefly describe the manufacturing process and how the protocol used for the study pertains to the process and how it relates to the validation master plan.*

Objective   *In this section, describe the type of validation study—for instance, installation, process performance, or product performance. Describe what information was to be learned from the study and in what ways that information is important.*

Summary   *In this section, summarize the design of the study. Describe how many trials or production runs were performed, how many units were tested, and whether the data support the criteria in the validation protocol. Explain whether there were any deviations from the study protocol and, if there were, whether they invalidated the study. (Deviations may have been due to improperly calibrated test and monitoring equipment.)*

Conclusion and Recommendations *This section should describe the conclusions of the study, and whether study data were consistent with previous study data. Describe how the conclusions support the idea of continuing with the validation protocol or restructuring it based on new information. Also, describe how the information from this study supports the conclusions of other company studies and, if so, which ones.*

Note: This is important because companies frequently fail to take advantage of valuable historical data collected from earlier studies.

Required Follow-Up Studies *Decide if the study needs to be repeated and, if so, should the same or different parameters be used. If different parameters are to be used, explain what they are and why the need for the change.*

Data Analysis *Summarize any data that is shown in tables, charts, or graphs. Attach any statistical analyses, cross-referencing any raw data retained by research and development.*

Data Sheets *In this section, provide an index of attached data sheets, or reference the controlled document file where the data are located. Be sure to label the data sheets with the study number, the date, the name of the person performing the validation study, and the study number.*

Study Personnel and Dates *List the names (including contract personnel), departments, and responsibilities of all personnel involved in performing the validation study and analyzing its data. Also include the dates of the study.*

Actual Study Cost *Account for the cost of all labor, materials, equipment time, analytical testing, and statistical analysis. Be sure to include any special costs incurred, such as for waste disposal.*

Material Disposition *In this section, describe the way the material from the study was disposed of (for example, salvaged for other validation studies, scrapped, or sold).*

Authorizations *Indicate the required signatures (authors of the study, appropriate management, and so on). Signatures should be dated.*

DETAILS OF THE ISO 9000 SERIES ELEMENTS (CONTINUED)

4.17 INTERNAL QUALITY AUDITS

The supplier shall establish and maintain documented procedures for planning and implementing internal quality audits to verify whether quality activities and related results comply with planned arrangements and to determine the effectiveness of the quality system.

Internal quality audits shall be scheduled on the basis of the status and importance of the activity to be audited and shall be carried out by personnel independent of those having direct responsibility for the activity being audited.

The results of the audits shall be recorded (see 4.16) and brought to the attention of the personnel having responsibility in the area audited. The management personnel responsible for the area shall take timely corrective action on the deficiencies found during the audit.

Follow-up audit activities shall record the implementation and effectiveness of the corrective action taken (see 4.16).

Note 1: The results of internal quality audits form an integral part of management review activities (see 4.1.3).

Note 2: Guidance on quality system audits is given in ISO 10011.

Internal auditing, corrective action, and follow-up are the mechanisms essential to the improvement of the quality system. The thoroughness of an internal audit—not only in judging compliance with, but effectiveness of, the quality system—concerning corrective actions is evidence that an organization is committed to its quality system.

4.18 TRAINING

The supplier shall establish and maintain documented procedures for identifying training needs and provide for the training of all personnel performing activities affecting quality. Personnel performing specific assigned tasks shall be qualified on the basis of appropriate education, training, and/or experience, as required. Appropriate records of training shall be maintained (see 4.16).

Every employee in an organization affects quality, and appropriate training should be a requirement for each and every one. ISO 9000 requires continuous improvement, and continuous improvement as applied to training is not restricted to operations or manufacturing—it applies equally to white-collar productivity. Training can be past experience, continuing education, formal courses and seminars, and in-house classroom instruction. Training can also include instruction provided directly in a work situation by qualified supervisors and other personnel.

All education, experience, and training should be recorded in the employee's personnel record.

4.19 SERVICING

Where servicing is a specified requirement, the supplier shall establish and maintain documented procedures for performing these services and for reporting and verifying that such services meet these requirements.

ISO 9001 comprises design, production, installation, and servicing. Therefore, service operations should meet all requirements of the entire standard.

4.20 STATISTICAL TECHNIQUES

4.20.1 Identification of Need

The supplier shall identify the need for statistical techniques required for establishing, controlling, and verifying process capability and product characteristics.

If the nature of the process and/or product warrants the use of statistical techniques, the supplier should include in the process control and/or inspection procedures either a reference to an appropriate standard or the rules for the application of the statistical techniques.

4.20.2 Procedures

The supplier shall establish and maintain documented procedures to implement and control the application of the statistical techniques identified in 4.20.1.

Appendix

PART 1: ISO 9000 REFERENCES, ORGANIZATIONS AND SOFTWARE

REFERENCES

Bergkvist, Hans; W. Dean Hawley; and Alex Dely. "ISO 9000: Getting There Faster and at Lower Cost," *MAN Magazine.* March 1993, pp. 46–47.

Breitenberg, Maureen. *More Questions and Answers on the ISO 9000 Standard Series and Related Issues.* Springfield, VA: U.S. Department of Commerce, National Institute of Standards and Technology (NIST), 1993.

> This is a good booklet on the ISO 9000 standards. NIST is located in Gaithersburg, MD 20899. Phone: (301) 975–3771. They're also the people who administer the Malcolm Baldrige National Quality Award Program.

Dely, Alex. "ISO Certification in 12 Months," *MAN Magazine.* July 1993, pp. 32–33.

> Excellent series of articles by an expert in international trade and joint ventures. You can reach Professor Dely at (602) 721–4336.

Dely, Alex. "The 10 Most Common Causes of ISO 9000 Audit Failure," *MAN Magazine.* August 1993, pp. 52–53.

Dely, Alex. "ISO Compliance: Financial Costs and Benefits," *MAN Magazine.* September 1993, pp. 40–41.

Dely, Alex. "The Need for Real-Time, Non-Falsifiable ISO 9000 Compliance," *MAN Magazine.* October 1993, pp. 38, 40, 42–43.

Dely, Alex, "North American ISO 9000 Registrar Fees Survey," *MAN Magazine.* November 1993, pp. 38–39.

Dubbs, Dana. "ISO Who?" Facilities Design & Management. October 1993, pp. 58–59.

Hawley, W. Dean. *ISO 9001 Standards.* Tucson, AZ: Attexor, N.A., Inc., 1994.

> This is from the president of Attexor, N.A., sales agent for Nicodemus ISO 9000 software.

Hockman, Kymberly K. "ISO 9000: Opportunity or Nightmare? Are European Quality Standards a Barrier to Trade?" *ISO 9000 News.* January 1992.

> Note that this article, and many others I've read on ISO 9000, was "downloaded" from CompuServe Bulletin Board Service. You can reach CompuServe at (800) 848–8990.

PART 1 (continued)

Johnson, Gary L. "ISO Standards—Aiming for Global Quality," *MetalForming Magazine*. March 1992.

> From a reprint the Precision MetalForming Association sends out to people who request information on ISO 9000.

Kinni, Theodore B. "Preparing for Fast-Track ISO 9000 Registration," *Quality Digest*. October 1993, pp. 24–30.

> Description of how Bailey Controls won ISO 9001 and ISO 9003 Certification.

Landrum, Roger. "12 Reasons to Implement ISO 9000," *Quality Digest*. December 1993, pp. 39–42.

Long, Jim. "ISO 9000 Offers a New Way to Do Business," *EE-Evaluation Engineering*. December 1993, pp. 69–70.

Morrow, Mark. "Companies Find Savings with ISO 9000," *Quality Digest*. November 1993, p. 22.

> Another magazine you should subscribe to. Write QD at Box 882, Red Bluff, CA 96080–9904.

Morrow, Mark. "Has ISO Improved Your Work Life?" *Quality Digest*. December 1993, p. 22.

"PMA's New FAST TRACK Program Responds to Members' Interest in ISO 9000 Registration," *MetalForming Magazine*. October 1993, pp. 59–64.

> This article describes an ISO 9000 consulting package offered to members of the Precision Metalforming Association, a package similar to one I offer. You can reach PMA at (216) 585–8800.

Rabbitt, John T., and Peter A Bergh. *The ISO 9000 Book*. White Plains, NY: AMACOM Books, 1993.

> One of my favorites. These two guys know their stuff.

Spizizen, Gary. "The ISO 9000 Standards; Creating a Level Playing Field for International Quality," *National Productivity Review*. Summer 1992, pp. 331–345.

> Learn about ISO 9000 from beginning to end. An indispensable article for anybody interested in the topic.

Switzer, John H. "Coming Soon to a Company Near You: ISO 9000," *Xerox Engineering Systems DocuPlex Digest*. May 1993.

Teetor, R. J. "Finding Your Way with ISO 9000," *Tooling and Production*. January 1994, pp. 43–45.

ORGANIZATIONS

American Society for Quality Control (ASQC). 611 East Wisconsin Avenue, Milwaukee, WI 53201–3005. Phone: (800) 248–1946.

If you're involved in quality, you should be a member. Membership dues are less than $100 per year and there are local clubs all over the United States. ASQC is also the home for the Registrar Accreditation Board, which approves U.S. registrars. Call ASQC for ISO 9000 standards and fact sheet, list of publications, and information on their valuable publication, *Quality Progress.*

American Society for Training and Development (ASTD). Box 1443, Alexandria, VA 22313–2043. Phone: (703) 683–8100.

If you're a trainer involved in ISO 9000 and quality, this is another good organization to join. They have a quality special interest group and publish the magazine *Training and Development.*

CEEM Information Services. 10521 Braddock Road, Fairfax, VA 22032–2236. Phone: (800) 669–1567.

Resources for ISO 9000, including the extremely valuable *Quality Systems Update* newsletter (call for a free copy). In a new program, CEEM, along with Dun and Bradstreet, can also give you information on any one of the over 2,000 ISO 9000-certified firms. For more information on this service, call (800) 476–2446.

ISO 9000 Forum. Case postale 56, CH-1211, Geneva 20, Switzerland. International Phone: 41–22–749–01–11. FAX: 41–22–733–34–30.

An ISO 9000 users' group from ISO headquarters. It publishes another "must have" newsletter, *ISO 9000 News.* You can reach the editor, John Swaelens, through his CompuServe address (100112,3376).

National ISO 9000 Support Group. 9964 Cherry Valley, #2, Caledonia, MI 49316. Phone: (616) 891–1061; BBS (Bulletin Board Service) is (616) 891–9433.

Support group that promotes ISO 9000 certification. It publishes a newsletter, *Continuous Improvement,* and operates a computer BBS that you can initially connect to for free.

Perry, Johnson, Inc. 3000 Town Center, #2960, Southfield, MI 48075. Phone: (800) 800–0450.

ISO 9000 and quality training and consulting. It puts out a nice booklet introducing ISO 9000.

PART 1 (continued)

Western Trade Adjustment Assistance Center (TAAC). 3716 S. Hope Street, #200, Los Angeles, CA 90007. Phone: (213) 743–8427.

One of eleven "TAAC's" located throughout the United States. If you can prove your company has been "hurt" by foreign competition, you may be eligible for TAAC to pay for some consulting services, including the cost of ISO 9000 certification. The western TAAC Director, Daniel W. Jimenez, says, "This is one federal program that works."

SOFTWARE

Here is just a sampling of software available designed to help you get ISO 9000 certification. Most, if not all, of the software is PC based and requires Windows 3.1. Call the companies listed for more information on pricing and features.

CAS ISO 9000. Contact: Business Challenge, Inc., (212) 488–7038.

Billed as a user-friendly aid to learning ISO 9000 in the quickest time frame. Acts as an ISO 9000 tutor that generates an ISO 9000 action plan for you.

The Electronic ISO 9000 Document Control Department. Contact: Document Control Systems, (800) 825–9117.

Software that helps you comply with the document control requirements of ISO 9000.

IQS, Inc. Using your modem, call the BBS at (216) 333–4813. The phone number is (800) 635–5901.

Offers early versions of its software (calibration management, system documentation, customer management, and supplier management) as public domain (Free!) on the bulletin board system.

ISO Audit Master. Contact: Harrington Group, (800) 942–4830.

Eliminates the need for handwritten audits.

ISO 9000 Documentation Manual. Contact: TQN Publishing, (800) 836–3174.

Contains a variety of forms, documents, checklists, and so on, for ISO 9000 standards.

ISO 9000 Quality System Manual and System Procedure Manual. Contact: HQA, (219) 356–6092.

Documentation, checklists, and aids in writing your quality manual and procedures.

ISOXPERT. Contact: Management Software International, (800) 476–3279.

Software designed to help you gain ISO certification.

Nicodemus Gold. Contact: Attexor North America, (520) 721–4336.

Software designed to help you all through the ISO 9000 process and to maintain certification, once you get it. Has a real-time, non–falsifiable (RTNF) traceability function. Also contains all ISO 9000 manuals.

Powerway 9000. Contact: Powerway 9000, (800) 964–9004.

Makes a variety of ISO 9000 software including *Self-Assessment 9000* and *Quality Manual 9000.*

QA/S. Contact: Hertzler Systems, Inc., (219) 533–0571.

Software to make it easy to pinpoint product variation. Includes support for ISO 9000 standards.

125

ISO 9000

PART 2: UNOFFICIAL LIST OF U.S. QUALITY SYSTEM REGISTRARS

Call or write a number of the registrars and get their information packets. Interview them as you would potential employees. This is a partial list; for an exhaustive and up-to-date list of registrars, call the ASQC/RAB people at (800) 248–1946.

ABS Quality Evaluations, Inc.
James Ricks
16855 Northchase Drive
Houston, TX 77060
(713) 874–9564

American Association for Quality System Registration
John Locke
656 Quince Orchard Rd., #340
Gaithersburg, MD 20878–1409
(301) 869–1495

American European Services, Inc.
Eric Thibau
1054 31st St., NW, #120
Washington, DC 20007
(202) 337–3214

American Gas Association Laboratory Quality
Steve Gazy
8501 E. Pleasant Valley Rd.
Cleveland, OH 44131

American Quality Assessors
Frank Degar
1201 Main, #2010, Box 1149
Columbia, SC 29201
(803) 254–1164

American Society of Mechanical Engineers (ISO)
David Wizda
345 E. 47th St., 39W
New York, NY 10017
(212) 605–8713

AT & T Quality Registrars
John Malinauskas
650 Liberty Ave.
Union, NJ 07083
(800) 521–3399

AV Qualite
Terry Heaps
10497 Town & Country, #900
Houston, TX 77024

Bellcore Quality Registration
Edward Barabas
6 Corporate Place
Piscataway, NJ 08854
(908) 699–3739

BQS, Inc.
President
110 Summit Ave., P.O. Box 460
Montvale, NJ 076456

Canadian General Standards Board Quality Certification Branch
James Littlejohn
222 Queen St., Suite 1402
Ottawa, Ontario,
Canada K1A 1G6
(613) 941–8669

Davy Registrar Services
Leroy Pfenningwerth
One Oliver Plaza
Pittsburgh, PA 15222–2604
(412) 566–3402

PART 2 (continued)

Det Norske Veritas Industrial Services (DnV)
Steve Cumings
16340 Park 10 Place, #100
Houston, TX 77084
(713) 579–9003

DLS Quality Technology Association
James A. Kalitta
108 Hallmore Dr.
Camillus, NY 13031
(315) 468–5811

ETL Testing Labs/Intertek Services
President
Industrial Park
Cortland, NY 13045

Intertek
William Airey
9900 Main St., Suite 500
Fairfax, VA 22301–3969
(703) 273–4124

Perry Johnson Registrars, Inc.
Perry Johnson
3000 Town Center, #2960
Southfield, MI 48075
(800) 800–0450

KEMA USA
Theo Stoop
4379 County Line Rd.
Chalfont, PA 18914
(215) 822–4281

KPMG Quality Registrar
Daniel Brennan
3 Chestnut Ridge Rd.
Montvale, NJ 07645–0435
(201) 307–7000

Lloyd's Register Quality Assurance, Ltd.
Peter Stewart
33–41 Newark St.
Hoboken, NJ 07030
(201) 963–1111

MET Electrical Testing Company
Robert Ryan
916 W. Patapsco Ave.
Baltimore, MD 21230
(410) 354–2200

National Quality Assurance
James O'Neil
1146 Massachusetts Ave.
Boxborough, MA 01719
(508) 635–9256

National Sanitation Foundation (NSF)
Gary Puglio
3475 Plymouth Rd., P.O. Box 130140
Ann Arbor, MI 48106
(313) 769–8010

National Standards Authority of Ireland
Richard Bernier
5 Medallion Centre, Greenley St.
Merrimack, NH 03054
(603) 424–7070

OTS Quality Registrars
Andrew Bergman
10700 Northwest Frwy., #455
Houston, TX 77092
(713) 688–9494

Quality Management Institute
Malcolm J. Phipps
Mississauga Executive Centre, Suite 800
Two Robert Speck Parkway
Mississauga, Ontario,
Canada L4Z 1H8
(416) 272–3920

128

Part 2 (continued)

Quality System Registrars, Inc.
Marshall Courtois
13873 Park Center Rd., #217
Herndon, VA 22071–3279
(703) 478–0241

RTI/TUV
Robert Sechrist
1032 Elwell Ct., #222
Palo Alto, CA 94303
(415) 961–0521

SGS
John Brookes
1415 Park Ave.
Hoboken, NJ 07030
(201) 792–2400

Southwest Research Institute
President
P.O. Box 28510, 6220 Culbra Rd.
San Antonio, TX 78288–0510
(210) 684–5111

Steel-Related Industries Quality Registrar
Peter B. Lake
2000 Corporate Dr., #450
Wexford, PA 15090
(412) 935–2844

Testwell Craig Labs
President
47 Judson St.
Ossining, NY 10562
(914) 762–9000

TRA Certification
Thomas Arnold
700 E. Beardsley, P.O. Box 1081
Elkhart, IN 46515
(219) 264–0745

Tri-Tech Services, Inc. (Registrars)
Joseph A. Fabian
4700 Clairton Blvd.
Pittsburgh, PA 15236
(412) 884–2290

TUV America, Inc.
Manfred Popp
5 Cherry Hill Dr.
Danvers, MA 01923

TUV Rheinland of North America
Martin Langer
12 Commerce Rd.
Newtown, CT 06470
(203) 426–0888

Twin City Testing Corp.
President
662 Cromwell Ave.
St. Paul, MN 55114

Underwriters Labs (Quality Dept.)
Harvey Berman
1285 Walt Whitman Rd.
Melville, NY 11747–3081
(516) 271–6200

Vincotte USA, Inc.
President
10497 Town & Country Way, #900
Houston, TX 77024

PART 3: NEW ISO DEVELOPMENTS

New ISO Automotive Standards

QS-9000 is the new, highly prescriptive "Big Three Automakers" interpretation of ISO 9000. In September 1994 Ford, Chrysler and General Motors announced that QS-9000 would immediately replace all previous supplier quality programs. Several heavy truck manufacturers also adopted the QS-9000 standard.

The QS-9000 standard is divided into three sections.

Section 1: Common Requirements, which includes the exact text of ISO 9001 with the addition of automotive/heavy trucking requirements.

Section 2: Additional Requirements, which includes requirements beyond the scope of ISO 9001, common to all three manufacturers.

Section 3: Customer Specific Sections, which contains requirements unique to either Ford, General Motors, or Chrysler.

Each of the "Big Three" U.S. automobile manufacturers' requirements for QS-9000 requires that:

> Suppliers registered to an ISO 9000 standard without consideration of QS-9000 requirements shall contact their registrar and indicate that their customer(s) require(s) inclusion of QS-9000 in the registration process. The supplier shall update the quality system . . . to meet QS-9000. When conformance with QS-9000 has been verified, the registrar will issue a certificate citing conformance with QS-9000. Only registration certificates citing conformance to QS-9000 will be acceptable to the companies using this [QS-9000] document.

The minimum five documents automotive suppliers will need for the QS-9000 program are:

1. QS-9000 Quality System Requirements

2. Advanced Product Quality Planning and Control Plan (APQP) 3

3. Failure Mode and Effects Analysis (FMEA)

4. Measurement Systems Analysis

5. Fundamental SPC

ISO 9000

PART 3 (continued)

QS-9000 also includes several appendixes. Suppliers should pay careful attention to Appendix B, which describes the requirements for acceptable third-party registrars.

Because it streamlines and codifies the different quality criteria the "Big Three" automakers use, automotive suppliers should view QS-9000 as a help rather than hindrance.

While registration is not a stated requirement in QS-9000, Chrysler and General Motors have already notified suppliers they must be registered by the end of July 1997 for Chrysler and December 1997 for General Motors. What this means is that the majority of U.S. automotive suppliers will seek registration. To date, neither Japanese nor European automakers have not yet endorsed or adopted QS-9000, so their suppliers do not yet fall under these requirements.

To learn more about QS-9000:

For QS-9000 information and training, please contact:
    Automotive Industry Action Group (AIAG)
    26200 Lahser, Suite 200
    Southfield, MI 48034

You can also order the report *QS-9000: The New Automotive Quality Standard* from:
    The National ISO 9000 Support Group
    9864 Cherry Valley, Suite C
    Caledonia, MI 49316
    Phone: 616-891-9114
    Internet E-mail: isogroup@cris.com

New ISO Environmental Standards

As companies worldwide are working hard to qualify for ISO 9000 certification, the International Standards Organization is proposing a global environmental management standard. The new standard, to be called ISO 14000 when issued sometime in 1996, will include a set of voluntary guidelines and a certification program to help corporations implement a single, general environmental management system everywhere they operate. The standard will also call for corporate commitment to environmental excellence beyond national or regional regulatory boundaries.

Although it has no formal relationship to the ISO 9000 family of documents, it is structured much like the ISO 9001 standard. A central element of the ISO 14001 standard is the "Environmental Policy" defined by an organization's top management. A system is then defined that ensures that the environmental policy is carried out by the organization. This involves planning, implementation and operations, checking and corrective action, and management review.

Like ISO 9000, the new standard is voluntary and will likely become a *de facto* trade requirement (just like ISO 9000) to permit trade in the European Union.

To learn more about the new ISO 14000 environmental standards, contact ASQC or any other organizations or registrars listed in Parts one and two. CEEM also has a newsletter called the International Environmental Systems Update that might be helpful. You can order

ASQC's *Quality Progress Magazine and Quality Digest*
1350 Vista Way, Box 882
Red Bluff, CA 96080
916-527-8875
E-mail: qualitydig@qof.com

NOTES

NOTES

NOTES

NOW AVAILABLE FROM CRISP PUBLICATIONS

Books • Videos • CD-ROMs • Computer-Based Training Products

Subject Areas Include:

Management

Human Resources

Communication Skills

Personal Development

Marketing/Sales

Organizational Development

Customer Service/Quality

Computer Skills

Small Business and Entrepreneurship

Adult Literacy and Learning

Life Planning and Retirement

CRISP WORLDWIDE DISTRIBUTION

English language books are distributed worldwide. Major international distributors include:

ASIA/PACIFIC

Australia/New Zealand: In Learning, PO Box 1051, Springwood QLD, Brisbane, Australia 4127   Tel: 61-7-3-841-2286, Facsimile: 61-7-3-841-1580
ATTN: Messrs. Gordon

Philippines: Management Review Publishing, Inc., 301 Tito Jovey Center, Buencamino Str., Alabang, Muntinlupa, Metro Manila, Philippines   Tel: 632-842-3092,
E-mail: robert@easy.net.ph
ATTN: Mr. Trevor Roberts

Japan: Phoenix Associates Co., LTD., Mizuho Bldng, 3-F, 2-12-2, Kami Osaki, Shinagawa-Ku, Tokyo 141   Tel: 81-33-443-7231, Facsimile: 81-33-443-7640
ATTN: Mr. Peter Owans

CANADA

Reid Publishing, Ltd., Box 69559, 60 Briarwood Avenue, Port Credit, Ontario, Canada L5G 3N6   Tel: (905) 842-4428, Facsimile: (905) 842-9327
ATTN: Mr. Steve Connolly/Mr. Jerry McNabb

Trade Book Stores: Raincoast Books, 8680 Cambie Street, Vancouver, B.C., V6P 6M9
Tel: (604) 323-7100, Facsimile: (604) 323-2600
ATTN: Order Desk

EUROPEAN UNION

England: Flex Training, Ltd., 9-15 Hitchin Street, Baldock, Hertfordshire, SG7 6A, England   Tel: 44-1-46-289-6000, Facsimile: 44-1-46-289-2417
ATTN: M. David Willetts

INDIA

Multi-Media HRD, Pvt., Ltd., National House, Tulloch Road, Appolo Bunder, Bombay, India 400-039   Tel: 91-22-204-2281, Facsimile: 91-22-283-6478
ATTN: Messrs. Aggarwal

MEXICO

Grupo Editorial Iberoamerica, Nebraska 199, Col. Napoles, 03810 Mexico, D.F.
Tel: 525-523-0994, Facsimile: 525-543-1173
ATTN: Señor Nicholas Grepe

SOUTH AFRICA

Alternative Books, PO Box 1345, Ferndale 2160, South Africa
Tel: 27-11-792-7730, Facsimile: 27-11-792-7787
ATTN: Mr. Vernon de Haas